D1303080

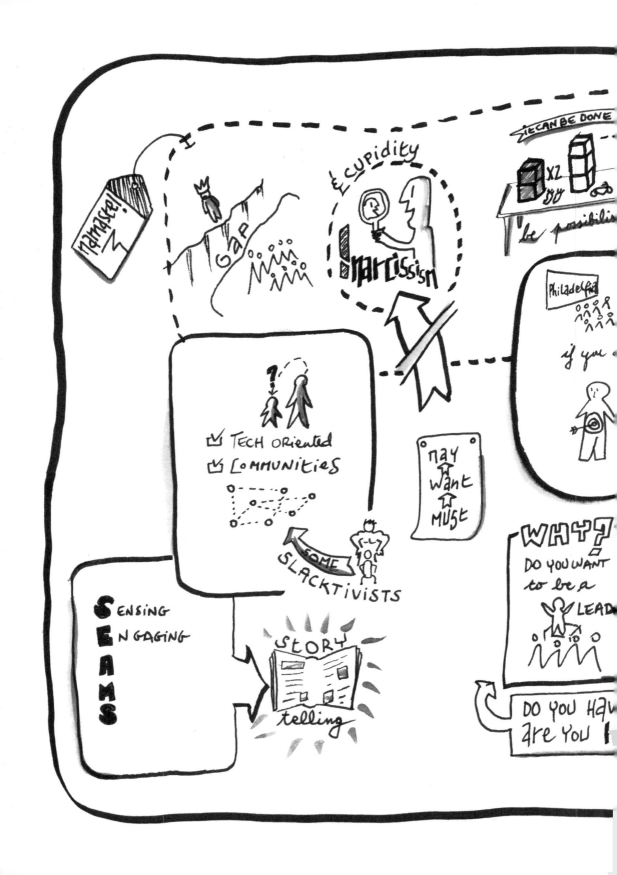

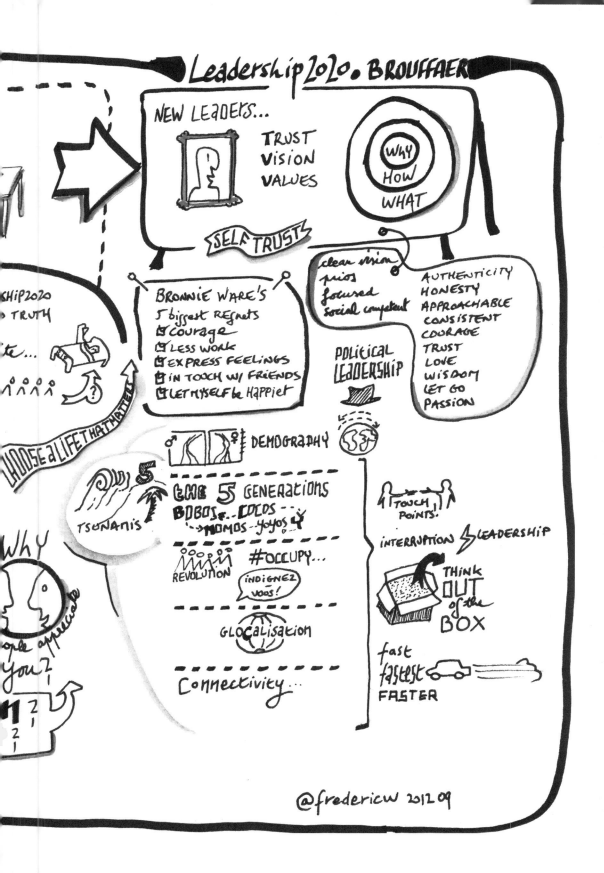

NO **WAY**

For Umar

Chaasti

29/09/16

NO WAY

THE BIG BAD BOSS ERA IS OVER

TRUST, INTEGRITY, HUMILITY

Bruno Rouffaer

LANNOO
CAMPUS

Second Edition: October 2014

D/2013/45/108 - ISBN 978 94 014 0816 5 – NUR 808

Original title: No Way – Big bad boss era is over (Dutch version)

© Bruno Rouffaer & Uitgeverij Lannoo nv, Tielt, 2013.

COVER DESIGN Uncompressed design studio – Frederick Feyfer
BOOK DESIGN Peer De Maeyer
ILLUSTRATIONS Frederic Williquet
PHOTO PAGE 20 *Denkmal 11, Museum of Modern Art, 11 West 53 Street, New York, 2008*
© Atelier Jan De Cock

LannooCampus is part of the Lannoo Group.

All rights reserved. No part of this publication may be reproduced,
stored in a retrieval system, or transmitted in any form or by any
means, electronic, mechanical, photocopying, recording, scanning
or otherwise, except as permitted by law, without either the prior
written permission of the author and the publisher.

Contents

Merci!

In May 2011, at the ASTD Fair in Orlando, I was invited by Agnieszka Chaber of the Polish Nowoczesna company to be a keynote speaker at the major HR Kongres Kadry to be held later that same year in Warsaw. The theme of my speech was to be 'Leadership 2020, the naked truth'. Dziękujemy Agnieszka!

That was the real starting point for this book.

Both before and after the congress the idea of writing something more on this important subject became increasingly rooted in my mind. However, I am not really a writer. Instead, I would prefer to describe myself as a creative, idea-generating storyteller. In the summer of 2012 I wrote down my story in a single sitting. For ten days I went into seclusion, living like a hermit on dry foods and ginger tea. When it was over, the book was ready and I was 10 kilos lighter!

My good friend Jan De Cock read my first story in our garden, and thanks to him I came into contact with LannooCampus and Hilde Van Mechelen. After an evening of wining, dining and talking in Leuven, it was decided to publish my manuscript. Hilde was convinced by my story, but saw immediately that at this stage it was only loosely held together. Fine for a speech, but not as the text for a book. Thanks for the trust, Hilde!

She said: 'We need to rework this story to make it more readable.' We didn't have to look far for help. Hans Housen and I were introduced to each other and we both knew instantly that the 'click' was there. Hans understands the writing business like no other and his ideas on leadership are fairly close to mine. The initial version of my story was too narrowly based on my speech and so Hans suggested a radical revision; a revision that would change total chaos into ordered chaos. We worked hard on the new text and on a Sunday morning in December we did a final run-through, almost like a dress rehearsal for a play. Done and dusted!

Thank you Hans for all your tips, tricks and above all for the way you were able to translate my thoughts into a readable story. Our discussions on the phone always helped to clarify matters and we were continually giving each other new ideas.

During this same period Toon Van den Brempt allowed his ever-critical mind to ponder on the different parts of my story. His idea to think in terms of 'acts' rather than chapters helped to give shape and form to the book. His suggestion to amplify the QR codes and his other innovative proposals were crucially important on several occasions. Thanks Toon!

Thanks also to Frederic Williquet for his lovely illustrations.

Linda, thanks for your foreword! Appreciate.

And then there are all my family, friends, colleagues...

Merci.
Bruno

FOLLOW BRUNO

on
Twitter: #brouffaer
LinkedIn: Bruno Rouffaer
YouTube: www.youtube.com/user/BrunoRouffaer
Email: bruno@rouffaerconsulting.com

Foreword

I first met Bruno about 2 years ago in Warsaw Poland where we were both keynote speakers at the Human Resources Kongres. It was there that I had the pleasure of hearing his presentation and spending time with Bruno. During our dialogues we realized that we shared a common mission and passion – building great leaders who can lead organizations to excellence. We defined excellent organizations as places where employees thrived, the communities in which these organizations were located prospered and they where sustainable over time. In our experience, there are leaders that were capable of creating such high performance organizations but there were also many leaders who did just the opposite. Numerous examples of leaders who focused on greed, manipulation of the workforce, a disregard for customers and generally exhibited arrogant behaviors and narcissistic tendencies can be cited. These leaders did not seem to care about the well being of the organizations they led. In some cases they even destroyed the value of once great enterprises. Newspapers and business periodicals globally are littered with stories and examples of serious leadership failures and acts of personal self interest. Our discussions led us to a common place - how to find and develop leaders who can lead high performance constructive organization that will be sustained overtime. We concluded in our discussions that there is indeed a new order of leadership is required for success in this next century – a renaissance of leadership that is based on humanistic values as a means to business success. This new order of leadership would embrace inclusion and a global view rather than exclusivity and a personal self interest view.

I shared with Bruno the research that was the underpinnings of our book *Winning with Transglobal Leadership* which I co-authored with Nazneen Razi PhD, Robert Cooke, PhD and Peter Barge. My co-authors and I shared a similar view although we came to this view from a different vantage point. We experienced firsthand the impact of globalization on business and leadership and were curious to learn why some leaders flourished in global assignments why others failed miserably or had marginal performance. As co-authors we realized that a global world was fast paced and getting faster and that it was unforgiving of leadership mistakes which became evident more quickly than ever before. Together we did extensive literature reviews and research trying to find the keys to leadership success in the global arena. We constructed a survey, tested it, refined it and survey over 150 successful global leaders and conducted indepth interviews to capture the "nuggets". We compared them to a data base of leaders we knew drove constructive, high performance organization globally. Through this comparison and correlation analysis we discovered what it is that set the successful global leaders apart of others. The key attributes that we uncovered can be summed up as follows:

Uncertainty resilience – the ability to make sense out of seeming chaos and create a clear path forward in ambiguous and confusing situations
Team connnectivety – the ability to connect talent around the work to innovate and solve customer problems
Pragmatic flexibility – the ability to respect others values and approaches and not impose your own on others
Perceptive responsiveness – being sensitive to others reactions to business approaches and needs and building bridges so that followers are clear on what needs to get done
Talent orientation – building and developing talent no matter where they are in the world and personally and actively supporting talent development – not delegating it to Human Resources

These points resonated with Bruno and we realized we were aligned in our vision for leadership going forward.

I want to underscore that I have seen many wonderful examples and exemplars of great leadership in my career and for that I am most thankful. My "hat off" to those leaders I had the great privilege to learn from. I have seen, as have my colleagues, leaders who are great in a local setting but don't have the desire or aptitude to branch out to new and unchartered global territories. I have also worked for and experienced leaders who generally are toxic and a disaster work for ---but from whom I learned a great deal. More importantly, I want to commend the leaders I have personally experienced who had the courage and conviction to lead in ways that engaged others and created cultures of positive performance and success. This is not easy - as anyone who has led others knows.

Leadership is a privilege and a never ending journey and I think this book highlights some of the truths of leadership that we all must reflect upon and ensure we avoid. Bruno offers compelling arguments for why leadership must change! His research relative to values and new entrants into the workforce is compelling. He offers of view of leadership that is thoughtful and thought provoking. He closes by highlighting a recipe for success that in my opinion can set any leader on the right path. Kudos to Bruno for a compelling, and at times uncomfortable book. It will take you out of your "comfort zone" and help you along your never ending leadership journey. Together with Bruno we are working on a Winning With Transglobal Leadership Program.
If you continue to aspire to great leadership this book is a must read.

Linda D. Sharkey, Ph.D
Business Strategist, HR Executive and Fortune 10 Talent Development Expert
Global Managing Director and Partner Achieveblue

Context

This is not a story about Utopia, but a plea for common sense. I want to invite you to consider a radical change in leadership. Why? Because the old style of leadership is destroying the future of mankind. Our economic, social and cultural structures and systems are in imbalance. We owe it to ourselves and to future generations to think seriously about how we can do things differently, with a focus on real and lasting sustainability.

In my opinion, the source of all our current misery and irresponsible behavior can be ascribed to three basic human characteristics: *greed, hubris* and *narcissism*. These three characteristics run like a leitmotif throughout the history of mankind. They are our Higgs particles: they ensure that man, far more than any other creature on the planet, has a negative impact on his own environment and on other members of his own species.

Some people will deny the truth of this image and will argue, based on their own narcissistic tendencies, that man is, in fact, a kind of super-animal, the only creature capable of controlling and shaping its environment to suit its own needs. To these people I would say that during the past 3,000 years man has only proved that he has an insatiable desire to rule over others and to dominate nature. In reality, man has withdrawn from nature. To achieve this dominance, a variety of different power structures and systems have been set up and perpetuated, from one generation to the next. In turn, these structures and systems have given rise to a particular style of leadership, which I refer to as the 'facts and figures business'. As a result of these unhealthy developments, men and woman have become paralyzed, frozen in a rigid straightjacket of rules and conformity. Fun and games are alright at home, but when we are at work we must behave like 'grown-ups'. Our organizations have succeeded in crushing spontaneity and creativity out of people, whereas it is precisely these qualities that are so important if we wish to live and work in an innovative, flexible and efficient manner. And because these organizations only have room for the rational, we take our frustrations out on each other. Hierarchy, control, power, structures, processes: humans are the most irrational of all creatures, but we continue to seek ways to justify our irrational behavior with rational arguments. This disjointed style of leadership has led to the plundering of our mother system: the earth. Yet even this most scandalous crime is viewed (by most of us) through the rose-colored glasses of pie-charts, tables and statistics.

People don't tell their boss what they really think because they don't dare. The bosses know this, but still prefer to carry on believing that they are doing a good job.

So what can be done? Is it enough that our leaders should put greed, hubris and narcissism to one side, replacing them with the more admirable qualities of *altruism, humility* and *balance*? Will this right all the wrong that has been done in recent centuries? No, it is also necessary to radically alter the system that created and conditioned these leaders. The story of change is, as so often, an 'and…and'-story. It requires both a macro and a micro approach. We need to adjust our structures (including corporate management and political decision-making) and the individual values and behaviors that attach to them. We must transform both these elements, moving them concurrently in the direction of greater *balance, empathy, fairness, trust, inclusion and long-term thinking*. Only then will it be possible to create an environment in which true respect can blossom and flourish, respect for each other and for the world of nature that surrounds us. It is no longer sufficient to take just small steps. We need a giant leap forwards. And whether we are talking about structure or behavior, it is vital to remember that human beings – ordinary men and women like you and me – are the fundamental factor in deciding whether our world will be a happy place or a miserable one.

But there is hope. The seeds of change are already visible. As a counterweight to the selfish, all-destructive economy of the past, new, caring and sustainable 'green' economies are gradually emerging – sometimes known as 'peer-to-peer' economies. There are plenty of new companies where people are still working as hard as ever, but where it is also possible to have 'fun' and where the staff are treated first and foremost as human beings, rather than just as units of production. There are some organizations where the bosses no longer have their own separate offices, where people manage themselves in self-governing teams, where the HR manager is now known as the Chief Happiness Officer. What's in a name? Of course, there needs to be concrete content and a concrete context for all these developments. But the basic principle seems to me to be a positive and progressive one.

The move away from greed, hubris and narcissism towards altruism, humility and balance cannot be denied, nor can it be halted. The question is whether the old way and the new way can gradually grow towards each other, so that Gross National Product can become Gross National Happiness. Can we blend the best of the old with the best of the new to create a sustainable whole for the future? And can we afford to wait any longer…?

HOW
DO
YOU
GET UP
IN THE
MORNING?

To the reader

During my 25 years of professional activity as a consultant and coach in the training sector, I have gradually learnt more and more about the nature of leadership. I have searched for answers to questions such as:

What makes a good leader?

What distinguishes a good leader from a bad one?

What influences a leader, and how?

Why does someone want to be a leader?

What are the core values of a good leader?

What do we expect of our leaders?

What skills and competencies does a leader need to possess?

Why do leaders fail so often?

As a reader of this book, I want to place you in front of a mirror. A mirror makes things personal. This means (I hope) that you will not be able to pigeon-hole this story into a neat little box, whether it be 'leadership' or some other scientific specialization. This would put distance between you and the story, and that is not what I want. I have no intention of 'salami-slicing' reality in this artificial manner. This is the way that leads to radical-ism and extremism. Consequently, this book is not a 'scientific' work, but is based on 'reasonable' knowledge. However, this does not mean that this is a book for 'softies'. It requires a great deal of hard work and perseverance to shake off the old, system-sponsored methods and practices, so that you can finally transform yourself into a good leader.

The holistic approach – sometimes in a deliberately sloganistic manner – offers a total picture and invites you to reflect. It is also intended to create a *Gestalt* – in the psychological sense of defining the essence or shape of an entity's complete form – of both old leadership and new leadership. And this is something that you cannot stick neatly into a pigeon hole!

In everything that a person thinks or does, in the manner in which he/she lives and behaves, reason and emotion always go hand in hand. Our brain works as a single unit, and not as a series of fragmented parts. For this reason, it is vital that we should attempt to de-fragment or re-humanize people, so that we can once again approach them as a *Gestalt*-beings: beings who – in a sustainable manner – are a part of the whole. Even computers nowadays demand that their hard drives are regularly 'defragged', so that their data is compressed into a single file. In this way, it is possible to create more space. Everybody has his or her own vision of what is happening on earth today. But your reality or my reality are not the only true and valid realities. Hence, we find ourselves faced by greater breadth of thought rather than depth of thought.

For the writing of this book I have fished in many different intellectual and academic pools: economics, sociology, psychology, philosophy, moral philosophy, cultural philosophy, history. My sources are management literature relating to leadership, art history and contemporary art manifestos, the crises of the past 25 years and their consequences, years of experience with leadership training and coaching sessions, conversations with leaders, colleagues, artists and scientists, the many journeys I have made, and life on earth as I have witnessed it. I will also refer with frequency to (TED) conferences, to the gigantic YouTube library, to Wikipedia and other similar sites. What you will not find is a series of academic footnotes or references to distinguished authors, with full listings of forename and surname, book title, publishers, year of publication, page number, etc. Of course, I will be mentioning a number of interesting writers and thinkers in passing, as an invitation to search further for yourself on the web, so that you can extend the scope of this book and let your mind ponder on (and wonder at) their often fascinating hypotheses. Hence the QR codes that you will find at regular intervals in the text.

The content of the book is divided into seven parts – or 'Acts' – followed by an epilogue – or Coda:

Act I contains a number of crucial questions for today's leaders.

Act II explains what modern leadership is and is not, whilst at the same time clarifying a number of popular misconceptions on this subject.

Act III contains several examples of bad leadership.

Act IV describes the common qualities to be found in most great leaders.

Act V details the forward-looking values on which good leadership must be based.

Act VI outlines the social upheavals awaiting us in the years ahead, for which leaders will need to find a satisfactory answer, if they wish to be judged favorable by their people and by posterity.

Act VII is a work book, containing a list of questions that you must be able to answer if you want to become a good leader, and outlining the characteristics and competencies that are generally associated with good leadership.

In fine

We need future leaders who are blessed with a high degree of emotional, mental and spiritual intelligence. Their aim must be twofold: to be happy as individuals and to bring happiness to others as a member of a community.

The system has cut us up into little pieces. Our existence is fragmented. Reason at work. Emotions in our free time. Meditation in the traffic jam or on the commuter train. Do you think that this is 'normal'?

Ever since modern man left behind his rural existence and entered the wastelands of urban industrialization, western economic development has had an essentially dehumanizing effect. People have become fragmented, cut up into little pieces, transformed into 'useful' units or functional objects. This is the Taylorism of the 19th century, which was so brilliantly parodied by Charlie Chaplin in *Modern Times* (1936).

The young people of today wish to return to the time when human beings were treated in a human manner. They want to move away from dehumanization and back towards humanization, from fragmentation to defragmentation. 'See me as a whole person' is what they seem to be saying. This does not imply that modern youth wishes to turn its back on the existing economic system, so that they can 'return to nature'. It does, however, mean that they wish to go in search of greater balance and harmony in their lives.

We need to realize that our fate is in our own hands. We are the architects of our own destiny. Who is sitting behind the wheel of your car? You? Or someone else?

Make a positive choice. Dare to write your own scenario.
Namasté!
Bruno

© ATELIER JAN DE COCK

Make your choice

A party?

'*I saw my reflection in a window. I didn't know my own face.*' These are part of the lyrics of a Bruce Springsteen song. It was used as the title song for the film *Philadelphia*. Does it sound familiar? Andrew Beckett is a brilliant lawyer working on an important case. But then the first symptoms of AIDS begin to appear. Andrew's career with a distinguished law firm is suddenly in ruins, as is his social life. He becomes an outcast and eventually dies alone, with just his friend at his side. *Philadelphia* brings to life in brilliant cinema the entire Kübler-Ross model, with its theories about death, grief and acceptance. And the music goes straight to the heart.

I often start my leadership presentations with Springsteen's *Philadelphi'* song, because it conjures up hard-hitting images that can be quite confrontational. It says a lot about authenticity, injustice, manipulation, the dehumanizing effect of the system, false values, etc. It shows us what really matters and what does not.

The first question that I then ask my audience is this:
Imagine that tonight in your sleep you are summoned to join the choir celestial. What will your colleagues spontaneously say about you tomorrow, when they realize that you are not there? And how will they behave? Will they pause to reflect on the vagaries and injustices of life? Or will they just throw a party and celebrate?

Consider the general feeling of sadness at the passing of Vaclav Havel, the writer, dissident and politician, a good and peace-loving man who guided his country through its partition with Slovakia without bloodshed, and later became the first president of the Czech Republic. Compare this with the images of the death of the former Libyan president, Moammar Ghadaffi. For decades he was praised to the heavens while he remained safe in his high-security compound. But once the revolution came, people were soon dancing on the streets to cheer his demise. 'At last, we are free of that murderous dictator!' A party to celebrate the downfall of a greedy, proud and narcissistic leader.

Streets of Philadelphia.
Think about it.
What would your colleagues
say about you if you were
no longer there tomorrow?

How will you be remembered as a leader?
Make a choice!

Act I

The
undercurrent
of change

A false feeling of control

In recent times, the Western world has experienced shock after shock. And the waves of change show no signs of letting up. In fact, they are coming thicker and faster than ever, creating ever-growing uncertainty. Before we have managed to solve one crisis, another is already raising its ugly head. We seem to be increasingly unable to cope. How can we solve the financial crisis? How can we save our banks from bankruptcy? How will we be able to pay our pensions in years to come? How can we avoid the impending energy shortage? How can we continue to provide food, shelter and welfare to a world population whose numbers are spiraling out of control? How can we put right the damage we have caused to the climate? How can we prevent the melting of the ice-caps and a disastrous rise in sea-level? How can we save the 270 million inhabitants of Bangladesh, who are threatened with floods and drowning as a result? How? How? How? And, above all, how can we do all this together?

Not with our existing leadership models, that's for sure! Not by pulling our chairs up tighter under the richly furnished table of plenty and allowing ourselves to be served by lackeys. Not by thinking exclusively about me-me-me or us-us-us. Not by burying our heads in the sand or by always putting our own interests first. Organizations, companies and countries that only think of themselves, driven by a 'what's in it for me' mentality, are doomed to lose everything. So, too, are the old-style leaders.

The current perilous state of the world is the fault of today's leaders. Where are they going to lead us tomorrow? And why do they behave like they do? Do they do it for themselves? Or for others?

The most important thing today is that we must seek to discover what we can achieve together; must assess what we can decide together, in order to spare our fellow man from even greater misery and to make everyone happier than they now are.

For once, we need to learn from history and pause to consider the dreadful position that the current style of leadership has brought us to: financial crisis, political crisis, military crisis, resources crisis, energy crisis, climate crisis. We have never been so rich, yet never before have we saddled future generations with such a heavy burden of debt. Has our hunger for more actually made us any happier? Why does it seem that growth is inextricably linked with more stress and more burn-out? The so-called 'wealth' that the West has acquired in recent decades has only been achieved at great cost to ourselves and others. The feeling of control amongst old-style leaders is false. They don't really have any control at all.

The urban youth of Japan are caught in a consumption trap. The narcissism that drives their consumption and defines their identity is incompatible with the needs of the labor market, which must nevertheless provide people with the income that makes further consumption possible! It is a vicious circle from which there is no escape. Read here how Japanese youth is suffering.

The world is sick: economically, socially, culturally and politically. Today we are paying the price for the centuries-long dominance of greed, hubris and narcissism.

Since man evolved beyond his original ape-like existence – archaeologists and anthropologists date this development at about 600,000 years ago – he has developed into the most destructive and most conquest-minded creature in nature. Starting with the Renaissance, this barbaric creature underwent a long process of civilization. However, we now seem to find ourselves in a period of decadence, in which the neo-liberal, capitalist system seems to have gained the upper hand, so that it now governs our environment almost entirely.

Jeremy Rifkin on 'The Empathic Civilization: The Race to Global Consciousness in a World in Crisis.'

Moreover, this dominance has lasted sufficiently long that it has transformed many of our time-honored values and norms. We consume, often without thought and without limits, but at what cost? Likewise, we make profit, but again the question must be asked: at what cost? No matter how much we make, it is never enough. We put prosperity before everything, including welfare and well-being. We all remain frozen on the same slippery slope, without realizing that sooner or later we will slide to our destruction. How long will nature allow this 'unnatural' situation to persist? Like it or not, man is a part of nature, and in the end nature will always win. With or without mankind.

7 billion others

Today, there are some 7 billion people living on earth. This number is increasing all the time. The French photographer Yann Arthus-Bertrand, well-known for his film and book *The Earth From Above* (with a heart-shaped island on the cover), has (together with Good Planet) developed an excellent educational campaign: *7 billion others*. Arthus-Bertrand collected 5,000 video testimonies on the themes of life, love and happiness. His objective? To force people to face up to the facts and encourage them to live together in a more responsible manner, with greater respect for the planet and its inhabitants.

'7 billion others' seeks to persuade people to take co-ordinated action to live better lives. The videos and the book force us to look in the mirror before it is too late. Highly recommended!

Taken together, these testimonies tell the current story of mankind, in a series of memorable images that are attractive, warm, gentle and touching. People from all over the world are asked some of life's most crucial questions: *What does your family mean for you? What makes you happy? Are you happy? What is your greatest fear? What is the meaning of life? What does money mean for you?*

Frequently, I play this cd-rom, just to listen in silence and amazement to the stories of people like you and me, from all around the globe. Some of the witnesses have been sorely afflicted by trials such as war, famine, natural disasters, bereavement and the prevailing attitudes of the local culture. Yellow, white, brown or black; male or female; young or old; Inuit, Afghan, Mexican or Belgian: it soon becomes apparent that in our deepest inner self we are all wrestling with exactly the same questions, emotions and worries.

The testimonies of those who suffer bring us back to the question of leadership. Why do they suffer? Whose fault is it? Why don't their leaders do something? Read the book and you will learn more. A new edition has recently been published. *7 billion others* will help to transform your view of the world and will allow you to gain a more transglobal, holistic view of mankind. Together, we can stop this deadly rat-race.

The calls for change are becoming louder

If you want to experience 'power', then you should visit the MAS (Museum aan de Stroom = Museum by the River) in Antwerp, where you can see, feel and hear a magnificent work of art by Eric Smeichim. Just stand between the screens, where you can listen, see, sense... everything! It is remarkable, if slightly troubling! And ultra-realistic! It is the kind of art that makes you feel humble. Hopefully, it will help you to understand what is meant by the power of 'the Old System'.

The thirteenth edition of dOCUMENTA, a five-yearly art event in Kassel (Germany), was a huge and coordinated indictment of the current order of things. An indictment made by no fewer than 150 of the world's leading artists, chosen by the curator, CCB (Carolyn Christov-Bakargiev). It proved again (if any proof were needed) that art can be both enlightening and liberating.

In March 2012 the Post Growth Institute published the 'Enrich List': not the 100 richest people in the world, but the 100 people who had done most to make the world a better place.

Each year Forbes compiles a list of the 100 richest people on the planet. It is one of the most widely read of all annual lists. It reflects the old system, in which material gain and financial wealth are seen as the ultimate expression of happiness. One man, Carlos Slim, seems to be trying to get all the world's power in his hands. He has a fortune estimated at a value of 50 billion euros; roughly the same amount that the 'super-investor' Bernard Madoff lost with his hedge fund in 2008. The inhabitants of the village of Tetela de Ocampo, 100 kilometers north-east of Mexico City, are all too familiar with Slim. For years, they have been fighting his exploitation of possible gold and silver seams in the area, which has potentially disastrous consequences for the environment.

At the beginning of 2012 the Post Growth Institute published a different list, with the meaningful title: 'The EnRich List'. This was no longer a list of the rich and powerful, but was instead a ranking of the 100 people who have done most to enhance the lives of others and make the world a better place. Obviously enough, this list does not use material criteria, but rather spiritual, cultural and social criteria. If you scroll through the list, you will be surprised to find just how many different ways there are for tomorrow's leaders to make a stand for fairness and sustainability: brilliant people with brilliant minds and brilliant ideas. The list is a source of inspiration, energy and inquisitiveness.

On which list would you like to appear? The 'Forbes Top 100' or 'The EnRich List'?

Martina Violetta Jung is a visionary business woman, writer and speaker, who is active throughout Europe. She seeks to establish a bridge between 'facts-and-figures- driven business' and the physical, mental and spiritual aspects of being human.

Martina Violetta Jung is a good, warm, kind and amusing friend of mine, who has returned to 'her' Germany (and, more particularly, Hamburg), where she combines the writing of books, articles and columns with the care for her sick and ageing parents. In her book *Erst sein, dann Haben: Der spirituelle Weg zu einer erfolgreichen Unternehmensintegration* she lays her finger on the wound of modern society: you first need to be, before you can have.

Martina Violetta Jung is not alone. There is an ever-increasing flood of people who would like to see things change, who consciously wish to live, think and feel in a different manner, who strive to achieve harmony and happiness rather than wealth, and no longer wish to participate in the greedy, power-crazed, narcissistic, neo-liberal, facts-and-figures market economy, where everything is subordinated to money and growth. Today, the calls are growing ever-louder that we must first 'be', before we can 'have'. This undercurrent is becoming stronger and stronger, simply because developments such as the internet, the smart phone, social media and peer-to-peer outlets mean that people are much more closely linked to each other than ever before. In the past, countries, governments, companies, consortia, holdings and banks were able to hide with relative ease. Not any more. Nowadays, everything is so transparent that it has inevitably had an effect on the thinking of the ordinary man or woman in the street. Thanks to social media and the connectivity that now exists between people via smart phones, everybody knows exactly what is going on in the world. It is almost as if we are taking part in the street fighting in Tripoli or Damascus. Movements such as the Indignados, Occupy Wall Street, Wikileaks and Cohabitat have swelled into a tsunami of disenchant-

The Cohabitat movement, which started in Poland, unites various experts, who are keen to go in search of new 'old' ideas to make the relationship between 'man' and the 'earth' eco-system more sustainable.

ment against the current world leadership and their hegemonistic domination.

The critical voices around the world are finding each other with greater frequency and the call for change is becoming louder and louder. Moreover, this undercurrent is more than just a youth phenomenon. Not convinced? Just read the manifesto of Stéphane Hessel, an ex-diplomat who is now a venerable 95 years old. *Get Angry* – or in its original title *Indignez-vous* – was first published in a limited edition of just 6,000, but has since sold a staggering one and a half million copies.

Stéphane Hessel calls on us to protest ('Indignez-vous').

In addition to being a diplomat and ambassador, Hessel is also a writer, former French Resistance fighter and a survivor of the Nazi concentration camps. He was involved in the editing of the Universal Declaration of Human Rights in 1948 and for many generations he is a shining example of struggle against the unjust oppression of peoples and nations.

Listen to the speech by Martin Luther King

In *TIME FOR OUTRAGE (INDIGNEZ-VOUS)* Hessel offers us the following reasons for 'getting angry': the growing inequality between rich and poor, the lack of press freedom worldwide, the treatment of illegal immigrants, the failure to protect the environment, the 'strengthening' of the French welfare state and the sad plight of the Palestinian people. In the meantime, Los Indignados in Spain have also been inspired by Hessel's book. Their protests against political corruption, together with the Arab Spring, inspired other protest actions in Greece, Italy and Israel. Occupy Wall Street and the wider Occupy movement are other offshoots that have made a significant impact.

Listen to the speech by Mahatma Ghandi.

Stéphane Hessel is a classic example of passive resistance, of protest without violence, and therefore follows in the footsteps of many of the world's other great leaders, such as Mahatma Gandhi and Martin Luther King. Their underlying message is that the leadership of tomorrow needs to be driven by a new ethos, a new *condition humaine* that will approach human civilization from a different perspective.

Where exactly is the problem?

The recent Rio+20 (UN Conference on Sustainable Development) in Brazil achieved little of fundamental importance. On the contrary, its results were rather disappointing. We read everywhere that the earth is 'sick'. Climate is becoming more extreme, biodiversity is shrinking, land use is too intense, the ecological footprint is getting heavier… The seas are polluted, and so is the atmosphere. Natural disasters are increasing, while resources are shrinking and the shortage of water is becoming acute. So what measures were proposed in Rio to combat all these problems? None, or very few of significance. All we saw was procrastination and politicians who hid behind their own national interests, so that their popularity at home would not be damaged. It was just one big farce from start to finish, a *place m'as-tu vu*.

Each year the WWF publishes the Living Planet Report, a scientific report that maps the health of our planet.

At the same time, James Henry, the former chief economist at McKinsey, calculated that some *17,000 billion euros* of wealth is being 'hidden' from the tax authorities by the super-rich. 17,000 billion euros. That is as much as the combined value of the American and Japanese economies. And, according to Henry, that is not even the full picture. If property is also taken into account, the amount rises to an even more staggering *23,000 billion. The black hole* really does exist, but sadly we don't need to travel to the ends of the universe to find it. It is right here. Right now.

The Tax Justice Network: 'The Price of Offshore revisited'.

Are these the great examples that the leaders of tomorrow should try to emulate? Is this the type of leadership we need? Who will act as a good role model for our micro leaders in the making (students), for the micro leaders in companies, schools, hospitals, institutions and political movements? Will it be the meso leaders (influential organizations, from trade unions to employers' federations)? The macro leaders of large companies and corporations? The political leaders of the world's countries? Is there a single university, anywhere in the world, where the leaders of the future are being consciously shaped within the academic curriculum to tackle the monumental challenges that await them? Alas, the answer to all these questions is 'no'.

As long ago as 1513 Machiavelli wrote: 'It should be borne in mind that nothing is so difficult to prepare, so dangerous to implement and so doubtful of success than for a leader to portray himself as an advocate of change. Whoever does this immediately makes fierce enemies of those who profit from the existing situation, whereas he only finds lukewarm support from those who might eventually profit from the new situation.'

There is an important undercurrent demanding a new style of leadership. Empathic leadership. Also in organizations and companies. To achieve this, we need to get to know each other better. Include instead of exclude.

However, I am convinced that the old style of leaders will increasingly find themselves with their backs against the wall, pushed there by forces whose power they consistently underestimate. There are more and more people who want something 'different'. They see a desperate need for a new model of leadership that offers more room for altruism, combined with a holistic view of what needs to be done; a type of leadership that offers more room for balance, dares to challenge existing shibboleths and wishes to explore new paths to find new solutions; in matters great and small, in companies and organizations, as well as at national and supra-national levels. This is the kind of leadership that can serve as an example to future generations. I like to call it enlightened meta-leadership or renaissance leadership, or (as my colleague Linda Sharkey once described it in a book): *transglobal leadership*.

Here you can look at 'Winning with Transglobal Leadership: How to Find and Develop Top Global Talent to Build World-Class Organizations' by Linda D. Sharkey and her co-authors Nazneen Razi, Robert A. Cooke and Peter Barge.

There is nothing to stop you from demanding new leadership and a new approach in your own organization.

There is nothing to prevent you from setting your own good example. And so there is just one message to all the Don Quixote's in the world: *Let's move!*

Act II

The essence
of leadership

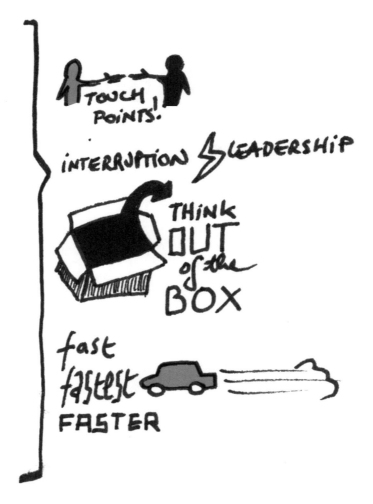

TOUCH POINTS!

INTERRUPTION ⚡ LEADERSHIP

THINK OUT of the BOX

fast
fastest
FASTER

Stop the clock

Always faster and faster, yet always more and more superficial. Is this the kind of world that people want?

Our world is changing very quickly. Everything is going faster and faster. And our leaders have adopted the same frantic rhythm.

As a result, in recent decades we have degenerated into a kind of 'interruption' leadership. Present-day leaders no longer have the time they need to do things properly. This means that they have less and less time to be in contact with their people, and the time that they do spend is becoming increasingly superficial, lacking any real depth or meaning. They are like an aircraft waiting for a landing slot at a busy airport: constantly circling, but not really going anywhere.

Ryanair pilots know all about this: land, unload, load and take-off, away to the next destination as quickly as possible. And if Michael O'Leary had his way there would be just one pilot instead of the standard two, with a trained stewardess to assist with landing and take-off! *Is this leadership or is it just greed?*

If I was O'Leary, I would remove all the seats and cram in the passengers like cattle in a cattle truck, the way they do with the metro in Japan. A crazy idea? Not at all! O'Leary has seriously considered the proposal, and all to the music of Tomorrowland, with payment for every drink and every piss you take. Find a hip concept, give it the right spin and away you go! *Love is in the air, guys and dolls!*

Is this modern leadership? Always faster and faster, yet always more and more superficial. Is this the kind of world that people want? Will it make them happy in the long run? I don't think so. What about you?

Leadership is about people

From an early age, from the cradle, in fact, we are all confronted with the concept of leadership: you are born as the first, second or third child in a family. Right from the very start, you need to fight to secure your own place in the pecking order: in your home, in the sandpit in the park, on the playground at school, in your team at football and, as you grow older, in every form of organization. It is an almost natural process. As a human animal growing up in a gigantic human zoo, we all of us, sooner or later, start displaying the qualities of a leader or a follower.

Non-human animals also recognize their leaders, and the older animals regularly need to make way for their younger and stronger rivals, even if only after a fierce fight before the whole herd. We are all familiar with the poignant image of the old buffalo or lion, who having lost his mastery withdraws from the group and finally dies alone, unloved and friendless on the prairie.

When I talk about leadership, I am referring to the values that form the basis for the actions and behavior of people with a 'leading' function. Leadership is about the way 'leaders' shape management processes and treat their associates.

350 years before the birth of Christ, Aristotle wrote: 'We are what we repeatedly do. Excellence, then, is not an act, but a habit.' What Aristotle was trying to say in his Greek way (in my opinion, at least) is this: real leadership is a constant! Leadership has nothing to do with playing a role. It has everything to do with the manner in which the leader interrelates with other people, whether they are 'important' or not, whether anyone is watching or not. You cannot turn leadership on and off like a light-bulb. You are a leader all the time, 24/7.

Perhaps you once acquired the competencies to become a leader, and perhaps that initially brought you a degree of success. Perhaps also, *en cours de route*, your environment changed dramatically, so that suddenly there were new expectations for which your competencies were no longer suited.

There are no certainties in today's world. Every kind of modern organization is operating under great pressure. Some are under pressure to survive, others to do better, yet others to innovate, conquer new markets, become more transparent, behave more responsibly… It seems that everyone and everything must be in a process of almost constant change. Organizations must be fast and flexible, so that they can react with a minimum of delay to meet new challenges or seize new opportunities. But when we use the word 'organization', we really mean 'people' and 'leaders'. It is these human elements that give inanimate organizations their resilience and adaptability.

It is the task of the leader to continually 'stir the pot', so that his people come up with new ideas or spontaneously suggest improvements. A leader must stimulate creativity and co-operation. And he must organize that oh so important resilience and adaptability. Leadership is therefore also about ensuring happiness, fun and play on the work-floor, since this is the only way to effectively achieve the desired levels of creativity, co-operation, resilience and adaptability. It is about bringing the best out in people. It is about the way you communicate, motivate and coach. It is about tapping the hidden talents that lie buried in all of us. Any leader who gives his people the opportunity to think for themselves and from within their own selves will reap a rich harvest. Only then will they commit to your ideas and give you their full support.

A good leader exudes dignity, trust, values and vision. He (or she) leads together with his people, rather than being above his people. This makes him stronger and it also makes his people stronger. A good leader does not mind when one of his team knows something that he does not. Quite the reverse. A good leader facilitates discussion, motivates his team to share ideas, and collates all the available information to reach the best possible decision. A good leader applauds when someone comes forward with an idea, even if it might not be immediately usable. In these circumstances 'Well done! And better luck next time!' is the right response, and not 'See, I told you so!' A good leader ensures open communication, creating an atmosphere of trust in which everyone can say what he or she wants to say, following which the leader must make and justify his decision. Because that, in the final analysis, is the object of the leadership exercise: to make the right decisions.

The balance between emotions and reason

In their search for efficiency and control, organizations have set up a wide range of structures and processes in recent decades. These structures are fed and maintained by budget summaries, statistical charts, powerpoints, targets and consultancy reports. The figures and the percentages allow an assessment of the company's performance to be made. And the same figures and percentages are also used to motivate the organization's people. Or that, at least, is the intention. All too often, however, it is simply a question of setting targets (realistic or not) and then telling the staff to 'get on with it'.

The idea that it is possible to steer and rationally control events is actually based on a false image of reality, rather than on reality itself. Human beings are emotional creatures. As such, they are not really well suited to the imposition of purely rational systems and structures.

Freud pointed out that many of the decisions relating to human behavior are made in our unconscious mind and are implemented via our subconscious mind, so that they are not influenced by reason (which is exclusively a product of the conscious mind). In other words, we often act without thinking. Instead, we allow ourselves to be led by our emotions: fear, anger, love, hate, shame, compassion, envy, disgust, dismay, etc. This is our unconscious world of instinctive desires and fantasies. This means that the behavior of leaders and the way they run our organizations, institutions and countries are also subject to these same non-rational influences, so that they likewise take decisions that are based on emotion rather than pure reason (whatever that might be).

This unconscious world penetrates deeply into the organizational culture of any community, no matter how large or small it is. Admiration and trust, jealousy and envy: a successful collaboration between colleagues will always be experienced differently by the different people involved, depending on whether these colleagues like each other or not. The efficiency of business processes and inter-departmental co-operation is based to a large extent on the degree of 'fit' between the personalities of the responsible people in charge.

You could argue that the management of the emotional balance within an organization is just as important for the general well-being of that organization as all its rational procedures and structures. In fact, it is almost certainly more important.

'One of the most important things that a leader must be able to do,' wrote Manfred Kets de Vries in his book *Leaders, fools and impostors*, 'is to sense the emotional needs of his subordinates and to take steps to respond to those needs.' To regard yourself as a leader, you therefore need to combine 'professional knowledge' with 'people knowledge' – and this is more a matter of feeling than learning.

You cannot learn feeling from management books or in fancy management schools. You can only acquire feeling by living in the real world, by experiencing real life. This means watching – really watching – what people do and listening – really listening – to what people say. Only then will you understand that you do not have all the answers.

In other words, you can achieve much as a leader by accepting that your people are emotional beings. This means that you need to possess both social and rational skills. If you can succeed in combining the emotional with the rational, and can move effortlessly between both these worlds, you are already a long way along the road to success.

The difference between leaders and managers

You can be a good manager, but that does not necessarily make you a good leader. And the opposite is also true. You can be a brilliant leader, but this does not automatically make you a brilliant manager.

This is the key problem with the classic companies that operate 'within the system': it is too readily assumed that managers can and will give leadership to their teams. However, it has often been drilled into these managers (in oft repeated company training courses) that their focus must be firmly set on facts and figures, percentages and targets. This means that most managers place a heavier emphasis on the rational. Their most important tools are powerpoints and Excel spreadsheets.

The question is, of course, whether this manager or expert is also capable of stimulating his people. Can he put the needs of the group before his own needs? Can he give people confidence? Is he trustworthy? Does he have the skills to get the best out of his team, to the benefit of both the organization and the team members? Unfortunately, these are questions that are hardly ever asked. Consequently, this is one of the most frequent and most disastrous mistakes made by present-day organizations: they make leaders of people who are unable to lead, so that everyone and everything suffers as a result.

What happens? The talent that the organization possesses is badly led, so that profits fall, targets are not met and morale plummets. People who are poorly led will only do what is expected of them – but no more. They opt for minimum performance, rather than being encouraged to give of their best. This is just a small step from the manager becoming a real 'pain in the ass', with stress, sickness and burn-out as a consequence.

A 'manager' is someone who 'manages': it is his task to plan, organize, allocate staff and exercise control over processes.

By contrast, a 'leader' determines the manner in which those management processes are guided and supported. In short, leadership determines the impact the processes will have on other people.

Many managers and experts are not capable of being a leader. They simply do not possess the necessary competencies. They have no empathy (it was something that wasn't taught at management school) and are emotionally illiterate. Most of them probably graduated *cum laude* as economists, engineers, lawyers, doctors, sociologists, psychologists, surgeons. But in all these courses of study you will find very little about how to deal with other people, with colleagues, with subordinates. As a result, they 'lead' in the manner with which they are familiar, with an emphasis on figures and targets, and by claiming to know more than anyone else in the group.

How do staff assess their bosses? The results of DDI research are revealing – and disturbing.

Too many managers are still unaware of their short-comings in the field of leadership. They do not coach, they do not discuss and they do not listen. Nevertheless, these things are expected of them – because most modern organizations have at least got that far! Any manager with a little ambition knows that nowadays the bar for success is set very high. You must be able to move fluently between different styles, almost like a chameleon, whilst at the same time managing by objectives, by wandering, by exception, by delegation, by walking around, by directions and control, by example, by strategy, by analytics, by listening, by process, by motivation, by content type, by principles, by imagination, by matrices, by processes and facts, by surprise, by generation, by spreadsheet, by definition and meaning, by e-mail, by destruction, by speech, by imitation, etc.

Does reading this give you a good feeling? Not for me. And not, I suspect, for many other managers. I imagine that there are a lot of people who are unhappy in their nice management jobs and wish they had simply stayed in the more comfortable world of experts. And I can imagine, too, that many others are still tempted by the ambition of becoming a manager, encouraged by the system but ultimately ending up in the same trap as everyone else. In this respect, many managers are caught between a rock and a hard place: they are forced to lead, even though they know that this will only lead to misery for themselves. Why? Because they don't have the emotional skills to deal with other people effectively. This is the fast lane to stress and burn-out. Result? Unhappy managers, unhappy staff, unhappy organizations, unhappy partners, unhappy families, unhappy world.

Very few managers are good leaders. Why? Because they don't know how to deal with other people. So do something about it! Leaders are first and foremost coaches, not managers.

It is worth repeating: a manager can be an excellent manager of organizational processes, but this does not make him a good leader. And vice versa. Managers who are also good leaders do exist, but they are few and far between. They do not grow on trees, and organizations must become more aware of this fact.

For this reason, I would argue in favor of the following distinction: 'make' good managers that can implement your organizational processes, but also 'take good care' that you have leaders/coaches, who through dialogue and discussion are able to guide, stimulate, motivate and facilitate your people. In this way you will not only ensure that your processes are moving your organization in the right direction, but will also help your staff to lead themselves. And this, after all, is a leader's ultimate objective.

Act III

Bad
leadership

NEW LEADERS...

TRUST
VISION
VALUES

& CUPIDITY

narcissism

A life of leading or following?

London. 11 August 2012.

It was sad to watch. After the victory of the Jamaican dream-team in the final of the 4 x 100 meters relay, Usain Bolt wanted to keep the baton as a souvenir, the ultimate trophy and a lasting reminder of this magnificent triumph in what will probably be his last Olympic Games. But even a polite and friendly request didn't help. The baton was taken out of the great athlete's hands by some self-important official. Rules are rules and gold medals are for memories – not relay batons!

It was more pleasing to see how this petty-minded official was roundly booed by the 80,000 spectators in the stadium, a feeling no doubt shared by millions of others watching on television around the world.

This incident perfectly illustrated the power structure that exists in top-class sport. The Olympic ideal embodied by the athletes on the track and in the field stands in sharp contrast to the power games that are played out behind the scenes, exemplified by the fossilized ruins who clumsily hand out the medals and flowers at each victory ceremony. It is not the Usain Bolts of the world who rule the billion dollar games, but the greedy old men in suits, relics of a past generation but still unwilling to relinquish the strings of power.

But perhaps we should forgive this elderly official. He was probably instructed by the big-wigs at the top to collect the batons, so that they can be deposited in the Olympic museum – to gather dust.

The only thing for which you bear absolutely no responsibility in life is your conception (that was all your father and mother's work). And it is likewise to be hoped that you will bear no responsibility for your ultimate demise. Between these two extremes, the alpha and omega of human existence, you live your life. A brief stay on the world's stage, hardly more than a nanosecond on the universe's never-ending timeline.

You also have no influence over the family into which you are born and the place where, as an infant, you will initially live. Nor about the culture in which you will be raised. The opportunities you will be given – with all the whys and wherefores they involve – will also to some extent be random; something that just happens rather than something you initiate.

This is also true for the meaning of words. Fetching something to drink does not mean the same in the wastelands of Ethiopia as it does in Paris or Rome. Going to school in an Afghan mountain village cannot be compared to going to school in Berlin or New York. You need different social skills to survive in Moscow than you need in Ouagadougou or Aleppo. The cultural environment in Dubai will have a very different impact on your upbringing than the cultural environment of a township in Johannesburg. Chances in life – whether for proper personal development or even for basic survival – are not equally distributed. You cannot choose; you simply have to be lucky. And so it is with the leaders that you encounter in your life.

Everyone – yes, I think everyone – will have been confronted with examples of bad leadership, directly or indirectly, latent or manifest, conscious or unconscious.

Innocence only lasts for ten seconds. You leave the warmth and comfort of your mother's womb, you hang for a few brief moments in the air and then suddenly… pow! You get a painful smack on the bottom from the gynaecologist, your very first leader! Man is the only creature that welcomes its newborn into the world in such a brusque manner. A baby calf finds its own way into consciousness, without the need for a helping hand (or hoof) from its mother or the vet. Likewise with lions, elephants, giraffes and a whole Noah's ark of other species. But not man. No, we are ushered into existence with a swift whack in the butt. Perhaps it is a sign of things to come. After the 'welcome' from our first gynaecological leader, we soon discover in the early years of life that we have a whole series of other leaders to contend with: parents, brothers, sisters, babysitters, friends, teachers… And it doesn't stop there: lecturers, professors, employers, partners, team leaders, managers, CEOs, doctors, nurses, care workers… They won't even leave you alone when you are dead: priests, undertakers, mourners… We are confronted throughout our life. And where there are leaders, there also have to be followers.

Sometimes we have the chance to choose our leaders; in many other instances we do not.

The anthropologist Ralph Linton distinguishes between 'ascribed positions' and 'achieved positions': an 'achieved position' is a place in society that you have earned by your own merits; an 'ascribed position' is a place in society that you have been granted by someone else, without the need for any positive contribution on your part. The leadership of a political party may, for example, be an ascribed position. If, however (as is often the case in Belgium), political leaders push forward their own children to follow in their footsteps, this smacks of being an attributed position. This is even more blatantly the case in hereditary monarchies, where the first-born child of the king is destined to succeed to the throne, even if he (or she) is an imbecile.

I have no real problem with achieved positions, as long as they are based on positive achievements and merits. However, if these achievements and merits are associated with greed or power – as is the case, for example, with rival mafia gangs in Sicily or competing drugs cartels in Mexico – that is a very different matter. It is impossible to reconcile these examples of 'leadership' with the altruistic and empathic leadership that I am in favor of. I also have difficulty with allocated positions, because the holders of such positions are predestined to assume them simply because of who they are, and not because of what they are.

Leaders destined by birth to acquire a place of power and privilege within the system have existed at all times and in all places. They still exist to day: in countries (for example, North Korea), in tribes (for example, the native kingdoms of Africa), in the business world (the successor to daddy or mummy is not necessarily the best leader) and in political parties (for example, the ANC in South Africa, which threatens to drown in a sea of corruption; as one supporter recently wrote: *Mister Mandela, from Madiba, member of the Global Elders Community: Where are you please, so that you could still use your great leadership authority to give these ANC leaders insight in what could happen to your beautiful country, my second home?"*).

Shit always runs downhill

When you join an organization, you quickly sense what its leadership is like; not by what people tell you, but by how they behave: social or asocial, smiling or frowning, natural or forced, open or suspicious, careful or carefree. In other words, you soon know if the leaders are popular or not, whether they are actively supported or just inactively tolerated. You can almost smell it in the air.

One of the sayings I use regularly in my workshops is the old cooking adage: 'A fish stinks from the head downwards'. Cooks always first check the head of the fish to see if it is fresh or not. The eyes and the gills are what interest them initially. Only if these are in order will they then move on to test the firmness of the body. If the fish is rotten in the head, no amount of clever cooking can save it. On the contrary, it smells and can make you sick. All it is fit for is the dustbin (or the cat).

> Only 50% of leaders involve staff in the decisions that affect them. Why? Because they think they know better. But how can the boss know more than all his team combined?

It is a useful metaphor. In my work on change trajectories in organizations, I often hear the complaint: 'Try telling that to the people upstairs', meaning the bosses in their offices on the higher floors of the company headquarters. Many of the things that are wrong in a company can be attributed to problems at the top. The way in which leaders behave towards their staff can make or break the culture in an organization. If the mentality at the top

– like the head of the fish – is rotten and if those in positions of power fail to realize this, then no amount of enforced change at lower levels will save the day. *'Shit always runs downhill'.*

Bad leadership does not mean by definition that an organization is badly managed. Many badly-led companies achieve excellent profit results. Bullying behavior can certainly make people work harder but it won't make them happier – and so the strategy can only work in the short term (if it works at all).

Psychological hernia syndrome

Many organizations are plagued by psychological hernia syndrome. If trust and confidence are lost and if negative emotions gain the upper hand, divisions will quickly appear amongst the ranks and efficiency will fall at all levels. This kind of dysfunction is something that can weigh heavily on an organization, just like a hernia presses down on a nerve in your back, causing you pain and discomfort. It is the ballast that can drag an organization to the bottom of the sea.

Forbes: 10 reasons your top talent will leave you.

If the working environment is shabby and dirty, creating a sharp contrast with the values of the mission statement that hangs in the shiny new frame on a wall in the manager's brand-new office, you will automatically create members of staff who come to work reluctantly, with pain in their hearts (sometimes literally). People want to be treated like people, with respect and dignity. If they are treated in a manner that is as shabby as their office surroundings, they will seek to escape through sickness (genuine or not), stress and burn-out. Welfare creation in a company has as much value as wealth creation. In times of crisis, most companies fall back on the financials, focusing on profit maximization. Unfortunately, this also leads to happiness minimization. Companies that pay attention to both profits and pleasing staff will emerge more quickly from the crisis, and will also emerge stronger – or that, at least, is my opinion.

If an organization fails to live up to its own values; if the leaders give the impression through their actions that these values do not apply to them; or if they act contrary to values that their members of staff regard as essential – values such as honesty, respect and trust – then people on the work-floor will react emotionally. This will inevitably increase tension within the organization, so that the 'rational' management processes come under pressure. Some people will respond by externalizing the problem, doing only what is expected of them, but no more. They withdraw into themselves and express their demotivation in subtle ways. In short, they become fragmented. Others react more openly and with greater hostility; they actively work against the leadership, seeking to sabotage their plans. In extreme cases, they will leave the organization, closing the door with a loud bang behind them when they go. This is the worst possible scenario. If a company is badly led, it is always the best and most dynamic employees who leave first. It is the duds and has-beens who stay longest. 'People join companies, but leave bosses!'

People are very sensitive for bad leadership. We like to listen to leaders who are genuine, who tell us the truth and who exude authenticity. We want to work for an employer we can believe in, someone who takes account of our personal values and whose own values and behavior are compatible with our vision of life.

Of course, it is not only the employers who think in terms of profit and loss. Employees do it as well: they are just as interested in self-preservation and growth. Bosses who are too concerned with themselves have a tendency to forget this. They do so at their peril. Members of staff who are happy at work will also be happy to work – and work hard. Having said this, a perfect match between the personal wish-list of the employee and the professional wish-list of the employer is seldom found. As long as 'playing along' brings greater rewards than 'playing the loner', most people will suppress their own feelings and do what the leader expects of them. Emotional satisfaction is sacrificed for money or power. In extreme cases, this can lead to a 'yes-man' culture. But when the member of staff sees an opportunity that yields an even greater reward elsewhere (or if the risk of damage to himself is minimal), he will not hesitate to take it.

Bad leadership disturbs the harmony and balance within an organization. It results in dissatisfied, frustrated and unhappy employees. It also leads to silent protest. People withdraw into themselves, show less commitment, do only the minimum required and keep their talents under lock and key. This is clearly a suboptimal situation; first and foremost because the 'bad' leadership is most likely to be 'ethically' unjustifiable, but also because the potential available to the organization – its people and their skills – are not being properly used or are even being wasted.

Numerous studies worldwide have confirmed that sickness leave, absenteeism, accidents at work, staff turnover, etc. are all closely related to the perceived 'misbehavior' of management and leaders.

The absence of trust leads to higher costs. Watch Stephen Covey's film: 'The high cost of low trust'.

Human resources departments in companies have resources and tools that allow them to measure the cost of a psychological hernia. Fraud, unnecessary bureaucracy, superfluity, waste, deceit, indifference, time-wasting, loss of identity, espionage, unproductiveness, theft, incompetence, mediocrity, conflict, litigation, loss of custom, staff turnover: all these things can be analyzed, weighted and costed. Add them all together for all the organizations, companies, government institutions, schools, etc. throughout the world and you come to a figure that runs into tens of billions of euros. Stephen Covey, who has investigated the impact of trust (or its lack) on organizations, has dissected corporate hernia costs in fine detail. Why not have a look at his amusing film *The high cost of low trust* on YouTube.

What makes a bad boss?

There are big bosses and little bosses. But what makes a bad boss? How can he create imbalance and dysfunction? The answer is always the same: greed, hubris and narcissism, to a greater or lesser degree. This manifests itself in dishonesty, a lack of respect, an inflated ego, a loss of contact with reality, the use of primitive defense mechanisms, etc. In short, psychotic implosion.

GREED: THE INSATIABLE DESIRE FOR MORE

Greed is the satisfaction of your desires: your desire for money, power, things, status, fame, sex. These desires are sometimes limitless, incapable of fulfillment. And what applies to individuals applies equally to organizations: more growth, more profits, more takeovers. In this constant search for more, the values that first brought success to the organization are often sacrificed.

Greedy leaders are easy to recognize by the following single characteristic: *it is never enough.*

I know a number of bosses who came to realize late on in life precisely what kind of damage they had caused in their earlier years. They now blame themselves for a lack of self-knowledge. But there are plenty of other examples of bosses who never come to this realization and continue to deny all fault on their part.

Nothing in recent years was as pathetic as being forced to watch the antics of the haughty ex-leader of a once powerful bank, who was forced to hide for years from the public gaze. Mighty Maurice of Fortis, lost and alone in a world that does not understand him. More pathetic still was his claim in an interview some years later that he would do precisely the same again, if he was given the chance to go back in time (which, fortunately, he won't be). As so often with greedy bosses who fall flat on their faces, it was all the fault of 'the others'.

If you want to become a modern manager, the books of Manfred Kets de Vries are compulsory reading. Just do it!

His (ex-) staff know better. Hundreds of them attended my sessions. It was pitiful to see how much misery had been caused to those who had been sucked in by the megalomania of little men with big opinions of themselves, who gambled with billions of euros that were not even theirs to play with… Shame on you! Perhaps at first they were only looking for 'growth' and 'scale'. But in the end it was only a question of more and more. Once the point of no-return had been passed, figure-blindness set in and their emotional detachment from the real world became complete, flying from one meeting to the next by helicopter, cocooned in their own isolation. Is that what being a leader is really all about? Is that happiness? Of course it isn't. Open your eyes, man! I would recommend any manager to read the fascinating book *Happiness* by Manfred Kets de Vries.

HUBRIS: THE ROOT OF ALL EVIL

Superbia – hubris, or arrogance, if you prefer – has been regarded as one of the seven deadly sins for the best part of the last 2,000 years. Jim Collins wrote brilliantly about hubris in leaders in his book: *How the Mighty Fall – And Why Some Companies Never Give In.*

One of the most typical characteristics of a proud leader is the fact that at some point in their career they come to regard their success as self-evident, as a personal right, as something they 'deserve'. As a consequence, they no longer see success as the product of the hard work of an entire organization in pursuit of a commonly-agreed goal.

Because proud leaders are exclusively concerned with themselves, they fail to realize that their success might sometimes be due to luck or a fortuitous combination of circumstances. Such leaders have also lost the habit of questioning their own actions and decisions. They say: 'We deserve our success, because we are so good, so clever, so innovative and so generally all-round fantastic!' They would never dream of saying: 'We are successful because we understand the things we do and why we do them.'

Past success can often blind a leader. Proud leaders think that they are always right and believe that they have the ability control events perfectly. For this reason, proud leaders are more inclined to rely on 'tried-and-tested' methods. 'It worked in the past, it will work again'. And they keep on persisting, even when it is clear to others that this time things have gone wrong. Proud leaders quickly lose the ability to pick up external signals. They also refuse to face up to the realities of the situation, still claiming that things

will turn out well, even though everyone else can see that disaster is imminent. They will do everything they can to maintain their 'unimpeachable
image' as long as possible. They are like gamblers at a roulette table: they
'know' that the numbers will eventually turn in their favor. Even if they lose
heavily, the setback is 'only temporary' and the smile remains frozen on
their lip – at least as long as other people are around to see them.

Proud leaders:
- *regard success as natural and well-deserved;*
- *claim success for themselves;*
- *display 'peacock' behavior;*
- *attribute themselves superior qualities;*
- *take decisions on the basis of their ego;*
- *allow themselves to be tempted by adventures;*
- *focus of 'what' instead of 'why';*
- *never ask enquiring questions;*
- *never admit to being wrong;*
- *cover up mistakes.*

NARCISSISM: AN EXAGGERATED SENSE OF YOUR OWN VALUE

We are all narcissistic to some extent. And just as well! Feeling good about
yourself is important to your mental well-being. But someone who is exces-
sively narcissistic and is obsessively occupied with their own person can
become over-ambitious, show a lack of understanding for others, behave
in a domineering manner, etc. This can have disastrous consequences for
their environment and those around them. Sometimes you can identify a
narcissist by just looking at him (or her): they exude a sense of exaggerated
self-importance. And if appearance is not enough, then all you need to do
is listen: they are constantly talking about themselves, seeking to be the
centre of attention. Less extreme cases can hide their narcissism in subtle
manners, and many of them function reasonably well.

'Leaders who are driven by excessive narcissism typically have no awareness of the justifiable needs of their subordinates and frequently abuse
their loyalty.' So writes Manfred Kets de Vries in *Leiders, narren en bedriegers.*
He continues: 'This type of leader exploits people, is insensitive and over-
ambitious, and often finds it necessary to belittle others. This behavior
leads to submissiveness and passive dependence, so that subordinates can
no longer fulfill their critical functions. It is only when they are confronted
with serious personal problems – physical decline, failing career, marriage

difficulties, an increasing sense of emptiness in their work and relations – that these people will finally begin to wonder what is happening to them and why.' Kets de Vries has hit the nail on the head. Every leader quickly becomes addicted to power, and that is when you need a 'fool' around you – but a fool in the medieval sense of the word: someone who dares to question you as a leader and help you to keep your feet on the ground. Preferably before you turn into an impostor! *Leiders narren en bedriegers* is published by Scriptum Management.

Narcissistic leaders:
- *focus on themselves;*
- *constantly seek attention: 'look at me, forget the rest';*
- *are egotistical and show little altruism;*
- *develop a personality cult, often to the point of absurdity;*
- *are incapable of building long-term relationships;*
- *are dominant;*
- *lack empathy;*
- *are never satisfied;*
- *steamroller over everyone and everything;*
- *manipulate and abuse trust;*
- *have no real sense of conscience or guilt;*
- *are haughty and arrogant in their use of body-language;*
- *hate people who are not fascinated by them;*
- *misuse others to serve their own objectives and interests;*
- *act as though they are more important than they really are;*
- *always know better;*
- *are unable to view the world from another person's perspective;*
- *never display guilt, remorse or gratitude;*
- *are highly sensitive to criticism: 'my way or the highway';*
- *dislike being alone;*
- *always need to have their own way and will persist until they get it;*
- *feel that the ends always justify the means;*
- *are always very suspicious;*
- *are inconsistent in their behavior;*
- *are constantly changing their values and norms in accordance with their moods;*
- *are constantly seeking to acquire power and control (what a surprise!);*
- *suffer from the 4 P's: perks, power, podium, pay.*

The leadership drug

Being a leader means, self-evidently, that you accept the task of leading other people. As a leader, you therefore acquire a certain power over other people. Some leaders understand and interpret this concept better than others. And then there is the problem of translating it into concrete behavior and actions.

All studies into the long-term success of organizations agree on one significant point: success is dependent on healthy leadership. And the reverse is also true: leaders who find it difficult to maintain a good mental balance are often single-handedly responsible for the decline of their organizations.

When greed, hubris and narcissism are combined with power, be on your guard!

'Power' is always dangerous. Every leader or group of leaders who remain too long in power and have no 'fool' to help them keep their feet firmly on the ground run the risk of thinking that power is something 'natural'. When this happens they often surround themselves with a flock of yes-nodding 'sheep'.

Power, in the absence of opposition or at least someone to make you think twice about what you are doing, works like a drug: it gives you a buzz and is highly addictive. Greed and hubris, particularly when coupled with narcissism, can make people do strange and unpredictable things. How many people do you know who have absolutely no empathy? Hopefully, not many. But if you give these people power as well, there is a good chance that their resulting megalomania will dissuade anyone from daring to tell them that they are on the wrong track.

Many leaders know how to twist the truth to their advantage. And more often than not, nobody says a word against them. This is one of the biggest advantages of wealth and power. They allow you to create your own truth and your own reality. Powerful people surround themselves with followers (i.e. sycophants) who will confirm whatever they want to hear. The *salonfähigkeit* of some of our elected representatives, for example, sometimes borders on the obscene! Devoid of scruples, many of them no longer behave as if they were 'elected', but rather 'anointed'!

And what the big bosses can do, the small ones can do as well.

But even 'big' bosses sometimes have to accept a 'small' role. It is amusing to see how often leaders who are tyrants in the workplace become as meek as lambs once they arrive home. Or likewise, how CEOs who are the terrors of their offices one minute (I like to call it *imbu de sa personne*) hardly dare to say a word the next minute, when the owner of the company pays an unexpected call. I have seen it happen so many times. Amazing – but true!

Putting on a false front in this manner is a widespread and timeless phenomenon; appearing tough and hard to the outside world, but all tears and insecurity once the door of their apartment closes behind them. I once worked with a manager in the Netherlands for a number of years. Professionally, he was based in Amsterdam, but he spent his weekends in Paris. During the week he was Rambo: hard, untouchable, inviolate. Once he was in Paris, however, he was transformed into an insecure transvestite, lonely and vulnerable in the anonymity of the great city. Was this simply a form of emotional decompression? And his behavior in the office: just another example of someone working off the frustrations of his youth on his colleagues? When you coach a manager, you quickly learn to sense these kinds of things.

Some leaders are so powerful that they recognize no boundaries or restrictions. In these circumstances, their sheep-like followers often find themselves in such a tight straightjacket of obedience that they are forced to deny their own true selves. This can lead to a whole series of unpleasant consequences: frustration, emotional volatility, drink, women (or men), self-destruction, power games, even paedophilia... Surely we all remember teachers who vented their inadequacies on their poor, unsuspecting pupils? And how often have we heard in recent times of frustrated priests who turned their unwelcome attentions on the children in their care? It even happened to me once, but fortunately I was physically and mentally strong enough to resist. Sadly, however, there are many who still suffer in this manner, even though some of them are now in leadership positions themselves. The 1950s, 60s and 70s have left some very deep scars, which will take many years to heal.

A little bit crazy

Parlons-vrai. Four percent of leaders are psychopaths, according to research conducted by Robert Hare and Paul Babiak in the United States. That is one leader in every twenty-five. This means that a significant number of CEOS are social predators, hard men with a cruel disposition, for whom emotions and other people are simply a means to achieve their own objectives – which are usually more power, more money and more status. They make it to the top because they are ideally suited to needs of the system or because they know how to exploit that system to their own best advantage. They are able to conceal their true nature, thanks to their charm, high-ranking position and manipulative powers.

1 in every 25 company leaders is a psychopath, according to research conducted by the American psychologists Hare and Babiak.

MANAGERS AND THEIR SYNDROME OF PSYCHOLOGICAL HERNIA

PARANOID

SADISTIC

OBSESSIVE
COMPULSIVE

DEPENDENT

THEATRICAL

DEPRESSED

MASOCHISTIC

NARCISSISTIC

Disturbed
personalities
of leaders

BORDERLINE

ANTISOCIAL

PASSIVE
AGRESSIVE

SCHIZOID

AVOIDING

Yet perhaps we should not be so surprised by this figure of one in twenty-five. The world is full of leaders who have lost all sense of balance and have become totally divorced from the realities of normal life; people with disturbed personalities, who are unable to relate to others and have a blood-thirsty, power-crazed lust for dominance. They can be found at every level and in every section of society, and, consequently, also in business. From the lowliest clerk to the most senior manager.

History's greatest monsters.

Human history is littered with examples of mentally-disturbed, narcissistic leaders, some of whom were certifiably insane: Hitler and his entire psychotic entourage immediately spring to mind, but we have also had Stalin, Kim Jong Il, Karimov, Nijazov, Alexander the Great, Bernard Madoff, DSK, Ghadaffi, Teodorin Oblang, Hissène Habré, even the face-lifted Bonga Bonga man in Italy. And there are still plenty of them on the loose: Assad exterminating his own people in Syria, Pharaoh Mursi crushing the hope out of the Arabian spring in Egypt... Just have a look at the images of this man on YouTube. Him and his Muslim Brothers. Muslim? Yes. But brothers? Every sign of resistance to their will is suppressed with violence. Is this brotherhood? Is this the freedom that the revolution promised? The people of Egypt have exchanged one dictator for another. Perhaps the rhetoric is a little different, but the cruel behavior is just the same.

Twenty quotations from lunatic leaders.

The list of such tyrants throughout the centuries is depressingly long: moguls, pharaohs, tsars, emperors, kings, popes, etc., each abusing in their own stupid, megalomaniac way the people in their charge. They are classic examples of deviant, sometimes highly individual leadership, but always with a huge (and usually negative) impact on the happiness of those around them.

If you want to visit Ceaușescu's palace in Bucharest, have a look at this film. Remember to read the accompanying text.

If you want to visit the home of an archetypal narcissist, why not have a look at 1,100 cold and lifeless rooms of the palace of ex-president Ceaușescu in Bucharest (Rumania). An entire district of the city was demolished to make way for this 'grandeur'. It is 82 meters high and extends a staggering 92 meters underground. Only the Pentagon in Washington is bigger. It is enough to make you shudder.

I would love to visit the International Criminal Court in the Hague and ask that other Slavic narcissist – Ratko Mladic of Yugoslavia – why he wanted to become a leader. I sometimes imagine the questions I would ask him. 'What did you like about being a leader?' 'Was it executing thousands of innocent Muslims in Srebrenica?' 'Why did you do such a terrible thing?' 'Because you could?' 'Because you wanted to?' 'Because nobody tried to stop you?' 'Because you had the power as a general in an all-conquering army?' If you just take one look at his photograph, you will know the answers.

Be careful with examples

Nowadays, many voices in the West are full of praise for the newly emerging economies and markets of the future. In particular, reference is often made to the countries of the Middle and Far East. These are areas where growth is measured in double figures, rather than decimal points. People work hard, plans are realized quickly and efficiently, and bureaucratic restrictions are almost non-existent. Ambitions, like many of the new buildings in these countries, are running high. Very high indeed. These emerging economies seem to be in a competition to see who can pour the biggest amount of concrete in the shortest period of time. A new ring road around Shanghai? Sure, ready next month! (Although we first need to finish the one we started six months ago). A new airport for Delhi? A piece of cake! How many runways would you like?

Have you every been to Dubai?

If anywhere in the world epitomizes decadence and pure nihilism, Dubai is that place. But the financial crisis has hit the oil-rich Gulf state hard. Dubai is on the point of becoming a ghost town, a luxury haven for those who have billions rather than millions in their hidden bank accounts. Most Europeans who work there only manage to last a year, or two at most: they then 'take the money and run'. Over a period of three years I have a carried out several assignments there for a client-friend. During this time I have seen giant skyscrapers – more than one – rise from nothing to operational completion in just 9 months. The builders work day and night, often in temperatures of between 40 and 50 degrees. No wonder Dubai is sometimes called 'the killing fields of Arabia'. The lucky ones get put on the night shift: then the temperature drops to a refreshing 30 to 40 degrees! Dubai is a cold, soulless, megalomaniac project of mind-boggling proportions.

Even my friend, who was the top man in an international organization, has returned. What was his problem? Above all, the manner in which he was treated by the mega-rich sheiks: 'They treat you like dirt' (although in Dubai 'like dust' might be more appropriate). It is a sentiment that would probably be shared by the many thousands of Indians working in the building sector. Is this leadership in the 21st century? It seems more like the 10th century, BC.

Surely we can expect more than this from today's leaders? In the very different (and very social) world of ants such a thing could never happen. If an ant colony needs to cross a river, the young ants are rolled into the centre of an ant ball. The older generations then add successive layers to the ball in order of age, so that the oldest ants are on the outside. Only then does the ant colony enter the water. The older ants are often washed away and die. But the young ants, safe in the centre, ensure that the colony will survive. In our world, the rich and powerful would be at the centre of the ball, with the young, poor and weak on the outside. Just like on the *Titanic*. And with the same tragic results.

In 2010 Foxconn was under serious media pressure following a wave of suicides amongst its workers. SACOM (Students and Scholars Against Corporate Misbehavior) visited Foxconn's iPad production site in Chengdu to check if Foxconn and Apple were keeping their promises to provide decent working conditions in their factories.

Journalists are also 'leaders'. They can reach huge numbers of people with their words and are therefore capable of exercising influence for good or ill. Journalists therefore have power. And you might reasonably expect that they would exercise this power objectively, in order to bring people the truth. Why? Because we live in a world where things are no longer what they seem. Photographs and images can lend added weight to the credibility of the written word. However, I recently came across an example of a journalist who deliberately, and with premeditation, set out to distort the truth. I am referring to Brian Walski and his manipulated photographs of a family of Syrian refugees. The two photographs on the left were photoshopped to create the single photograph on the right, which appeared on the front page of *The Los Angeles Times* on 31 March 2012. After the trickery became known, the man was (quite rightly) dismissed from his job.

Who are you Brian? What are you looking for? Eternal fame?

The same kind of deceit hides behind the flashy facades of many of the world's most famous companies. What can we say about the Foxconn concentration camp – sorry, I mean 'factory' – in the Chinese city of Chengdu, where Apple makes most of its products? Most of the prisoners – sorry, I

Worldwide there are some 215 million children being exploited in child labor.

mean 'employees' – have to work at least 12 hours a day for 13 straight days before they are given a day off. This means 80 to 100 hours of compulsory overtime each month. What's more, they are forbidden to talk and are exposed to aluminum dust without adequate protection. All their work is done standing and sometimes they even need to skip meals, if they are behind on their production targets. Who is to blame for this appalling situation? Did Steve Jobs not see (or want to know) what was going on? Isolated from the real world? Just another 'far-from-my-bed' show?

And what about Ikea, which is chopping down thousands of acres of beautiful forest in north-west Russia (Kirelia) to make its furniture?

Or the bankers in suits, who gamble away the hard-earned money of others on high-risk investments?

Or the political leaders of southern Europe, who got their financial calculations wrong, so that they had to borrow huge (and unrepayable) amounts of money to keep their heads temporarily above water?

Or the company leaders who allow their products to be made by children? Their excuse? The oldest one in the book: *Wir haben es nicht gewusst.*

The conventions drawn up by the International Labor Organization (ILO) are amongst the most widely ratified conventions in the world. Nevertheless, there are still some 215 million children who are being exploited as cheap labor, often in the most appalling conditions. In Asia, Africa, Latin America. They do not go to school and are robbed of the chance to actually be children. More than half of all child labor is carried out in dangerous circumstances. According to the ILO, every minute of every day a child somewhere in the world is being injured, traumatized or made sick as a result of this despicable practice. 'It is true that the total number of children working in the world has fallen, but the categories between 15 and 17 years of age has grown by 20 percent… Although progress has been made during the past 10 years, the number of children working worldwide is still much too high,' says ILO boss Juan Somavia. 'Child labor is a clear indictment of the current growth model. We need to take urgent action with regard to work that endangers the health and safety of our children.' The objective of the ILO is to eliminate the worst forms of child labor by 2016, but I fear that the current economic crisis will seriously hamper this noble aspiration.

Is this modern leadership?

Why not do the test? The preamble of the United Nations Charter states: 'We, the peoples of the United Nations, are determined to save future generations from the scourge of war that has brought untold misery to mankind twice in our lifetime; to reaffirm faith in fundamental human rights, in the dignity and worth of the human person, in the equal rights of men and women and of nations large and small; to establish conditions under which justice and respect for obligations arising from treaties and other sources of international law can be maintained; and to promote social progress and better standards of life in larger freedom.'

Now look at the list of member states of the United Nations. Scroll through the list and note the year in which each country became a member. With these details at your disposal, you can check to see where war is still being fought; where countries are in financial difficulties; where dictators, great or small, are still clinging on to power. Or you can check which countries are setting a good example or are at least working at sustainable projects. Or which countries have produced great leaders. Or where infant mortality is declining. Or where the numbers attending education are increasing. Or who has an army and who does not?

The member states of the United Nations.

Every country will have leaders of some kind, leaders that have been chosen by the country itself (assuming that the people are allowed to choose). The wealth and welfare of a country is inextricably linked to this leadership issue. The key question is this: what message are the leaders giving and what values are they promoting? Where are they leading their people? Where are they leading the world, both now and in the long term? We need to find the answers to these questions, for the sake of our children and our children's children.

The list of countries without an army.

And what does all this say about our own society and our slavish addiction to globalized consumption? A society in which we want a new smart phone each year, a new interior every three years and a new car every four years (if not sooner); with twenty suits and sixty pairs of shoes in the closet, and a television in every room; where shopping is a leisure activity and five holidays a year are a must. *Do we care? Do we really care?* When will we change our consumerist behavior, so that others less fortunate than ourselves can also benefit?

Act IV

Good
leadership

HOW
WHAT

clear vision
prios
focused
social competent

AUTHENTICITY
HONESTY
APPROACHABLE
CONSISTENT
COURAGE
TRUST
LOVE
WISDOM
LET GO
PASSION

GAP

Chameleons

Management guru Paul Hersey once wrote the following: 'The style of leadership is determined by the image that others have of the leader. It is not the way people see themselves that counts, but rather the manner in which they are seen by those they are trying to influence. People don't know what you are thinking or feeling; they only see your behavior. When you think that you are being human and attentive, but your people find you hard and authoritarian, it is their perception, and not yours, that will determine their attitude and reaction.'

The message is clear: it is others who decide whether you are a good leader or not. And this assessment is not dependent on your qualifications and the make of your company car, but on your behavior, day after day. It is never the other way around. The child in the other person, whether he/she is your subordinate, colleague or boss, always speaks the truth.

Many people are trapped in a cage. Leaders too. They are locked into the system that created them. But does this lead to happiness?

People are like chameleons; they adjust themselves to the circumstances that have been created for them. The same is true of leaders; they adjust themselves to the environment that the system has created for them. In other words, the system creates leaders in its own image. Pyramid-structured companies with rational systems and procedures therefore like rational managers. This type of company will eventually grind – or rust – to a standstill. And the people who work there will rust away as well.

In 1936 Charlie Chaplin was already mocking this kind of Taylorism in his film *Modern Times*. Working on the chain gang – and with the soul in chains as well. This type of organization still exists today. And they are always moaning that they can't beat the competition, notwithstanding all their efficiency efforts. But the reason for their failure is obvious: they always put figures before people, and those people have also been 'forbidden' for years from being innovative or creative. Frederick Taylor, you have a lot to answer for!

We need to give staff their dignity back, so that they can once again come to work with pleasure. Happy employees are better employees: they work harder and are more efficient. They do more with less. Of course, there will no doubt be some MBA and ISO-certificated PPT adepts who think that the efficiency and effectiveness of happiness still needs to be proven. For my part, you can drop these spoilsports on a desert island with all the other moaners and groaners.

Reflections

Good leadership is based on harmony. It is about respecting the individual values of the people you work with. Values such as honesty, authenticity, active listening, reasonableness, consideration, openness, etc. We can speak of good leadership when the values displayed by the leader in his attitude and actions agree with the values that his people can find back in themselves, the values in which they believe and by which they live. If someone values honesty and respect, he will expect to find these values in his/her boss and in the organization for which he/she works. And if a person possesses a particular talent, they will find it pleasant to be able to make use of that talent at work. Good leaders are first and foremost men and women who empathize, who like to understand and take account of the things that are important to others, and who can translate that human concern into the productive environment of a business setting.

If we don't know whether [aid is] doing any good, we are no better than the medieval doctors with their leeches. (Esther Duflo)

Everyone knows the great leaders of recent times, the leaders who were really able to make a difference. I admire people such as Mahatma Gandhi, Nelson Mandela, Douglas Conant, the Dalai Lama, Indira Gandhi, Ana Azara, Hassan Bin Tahal, Noam Chomsky, JFK, Rifkin, Kofi Anan, Ai Weiwei, Luc Tuymans, Koen Van Mechelen, Jan De Cock and Ester Deflo, as well as many other teachers, professors and business managers from my professional past, to name but a few…

What these people all have in common is a burning and inextinguishable passion for their cause. But that's not all. They are also people who give, rather than take. People who first 'are', before they can 'have'. People who are concerned for the welfare of others and are conscious that their decisions have an impact on these others. People who challenge those around them to question their own self-interests and focus instead on the general good.

Consider, for example, the person of Aung San Suu Kyi, the leader of the peaceful movement for human rights and democracy in Myanmar. If you want to see how active and influential she has been, all you need to do is glance at the history of Burma/Myanmar over the past 30 years. Aung San Suu Kyi is an exceptionally strong woman and a textbook example of a true and honest leader. She is humble, generous and humane, and has an unshakeable faith in the rightness of her ideas. To such an extent that she was prepared to offer up her freedom for her ideals. Aung San Suu Kyi still has an uneasy relationship with the military regime, which possesses all power (and particularly economic power) in Myanmar. As so often, the happy few have everything and the have-nots are left to fend for themselves. Or they would be, were it not for the efforts of Aung San Suu Kyi. *Chapeau, il faut le faire.*

As a result of her efforts and sacrifices, she has built up an impressive CV, crammed with honors and titles from around the world, clear signs of international recognition and approval. Wikipedia gives the following list of awards. They make my personal appreciation of this ethical leader deeper than it already was:

- *Honorary Fellow of St Hugh's College (Oxford, UK) 1990*
- *Thorolf Rafto Human Rights Award (Norway) 1990*
- *Sacharov Prize for Freedom of Thought (European Parliament) 1990*
- *Nobel Prize for Peace (Oslo, Norway) 1991*
- *Honorary member, PEN International (Norwegian Centre) 1991*
- *Humanities Human Rights Award (USA) 1991*
- *Honorary member, PEN International (Canadian Centre) 1991*
- *Marisa Bellisario (Italy) 1992*
- *Annual award by the International Human Rights Law Group (USA) 1992*
- *Honorary member, PEN International (English Centre) 1992*
- *Simon Bolivar International Award (UNESCO) 1992*
- *Prix Litteraire des Droits de l'Homme Nouveaux (France) 1992*
- *Honorary member of the World Commission for Culture and Development (UNESCO) 1992*
- *Member of the Universal Cultural Academy (Paris, France) 1993*
- *International Forum of the Danish Labor Movement (Copenhagen, Denmark) 1993*
- *Victor Jara International Human Rights Centre for Human and Constitutional Rights, (Los Angeles, USA) 1993*
- *Member of the advisory council of the Francois-Xavier Bagnoud Centre for Health and Human Rights, Harvard University (USA) 1993*
- *Honorary adviser to the Forum of Democratic Leaders in Asia-Pacific, 1994*
- *Liberal International Prize for Freedom of Britain's Liberal Democrat Party (UK) 1995*

- *Jawaharlal Nehru Award for International Understanding (India) 1993*
- *IRC Freedom Award from the International Rescue Commission, 1995*
- *Companion of the Order of Australia, 1996*
- *W. Averell Harrimen Democracy Award, (US) 1996*
- *Rajiv Gandhi Memorial Award, (India) 1996*
- *Honorary doctorate, Cambridge University (UK) 1998*
- *Presidential Medal for Freedom (Washington, USA) 2000*
- *Madanjeet Singh Prize (UNESCO) 2002*
- *Olof Palme Prize, (Norway) 2005*
- *Freedom from Fear Medal, Roosevelt Foundation (The Netherlands) 2006*

A large number of other honorary degrees and honorary citizenships from various cities have been left out of this list, which would otherwise be longer and even more impressive. Nevertheless, it still runs to almost two pages. I am dumbfounded at the thought of it. And yet this great lady still remains as humble as ever, while our petty regional presidents and premiers still fight to see who will be first to shake her hand or have their picture taken with her. Narcissists in search of another fifteen minutes of fame, basking in her reflected glory. Ugh! It's enough to make you sick. 'Of course, I was the first to blablabla.' This is hardly showing Aung San Suu Kyi the respect she so richly deserves.

Sofi Cogley is another lady whom I deeply admire. Sofi is a tremendously enthusiastic and motivated Australian who runs an NGO – Isibani – in South Africa. I support her work heart and soul through our aid project, Tomorrow4Isibani.

Aung San Suu Kyi and Sofi Cogley, each in their own different manner and on their own different scale, are shining examples of people who live and work for 'a good cause'. Just by 'being' who they are, they radiate goodness and condemn badness. They put 'me, myself and I' in the last place, giving priority instead to the needs of others. There is no end to their ability to 'give'; their selflessness and their empathy are inexhaustible. They are simultaneously both manager and source of inspiration; the one for her country, the other for her organization. Because that country and that organization both need to be run; require a structure that can provide people with the leadership they expect and processes with the follow-up they need. In short, both country and organization need to be led. The key question is: how will the necessary decisions be taken and accepted? In my opinion, it is vital that the manner in which this is done reflects the ideals

In 2005 Tris went with her family to work in South Africa. In Winterton she was quickly confronted with the problem of HIV and Aids amongst the local Zulu population. To meet the needs of the sufferers, she started her Tomorrow project. Some time later, she met Sofi, an Australian lady who was already a number of steps further with her Isibani project. They decided to join forces – and so the Tomorrow4Isibani project was created.

and values for which the country or organization stands. And in this respect, I have full confidence in both Aung San Suu Kyi and Sofi!

I hope that everyone has someone like these two women in their environment, people to whom they can look up and on whom they can rely. And perhaps even imitate…

Exercises in leadership

Time for an exercise. We all know a number of micro and macro leaders who really cut the mustard. Take a sheet of paper and answer the following questions:

- *Who do you look up to?*
- *Who has inspired you in your life?*
- *Who has taught or given you the most?*
- *Who has had the greatest impact on you?*
- *Who has touched you most deeply or left their mark in your mind?*

Now that you have written down a number of names, we can move on to the next step.

- *Why have these people had such an impact on you?*

I am willing to bet that these 'leaders' brought about a positive change in your life, that they put your needs before their own, that they supported you when the going got tough, that they gave you opportunities to develop your talents, that they helped you to explore new boundaries, providing positive stimulation and inspiration. In short, they made you happy – and a better person.

- *Do these micro and macro leaders have common qualities or characteristics?*
- *What do they radiate to others?*

I have done this exercise myself. With a list of great leaders whom I admire in my hand, I searched for common features that they all shared, things that they all possessed but which set them apart from the crowd. I came to the following conclusion.

Great leaders distinguish themselves from others by the fact that their thinking is not based on 'what's in it for me', but is motivated instead by an inner need to be of service to others. Great leaders avoid bad behavior, search for goodness, and try to find out the 'why' behind people's actions, rather than focusing on the 'how' and the 'what'. They do this by first applying this process to themselves, before they move on to others. In other words, they know exactly who they are and why they want to change things. In particular, the answer to the 'why' question is the foundation on which their later deeds are built.

Great leaders first question themselves before they question others. Searching for trust in others must always first be preceded by self-trust. Stephen Covey talks about what he calls the 5 waves of trust. Watch his YouTube film here.

Great leaders not only succeed in giving an answer to the great 'why' question but also have the ability to translate this understanding into an inspirational vision, which they are able to communicate in a charismatic manner. They are able to make others believe what they believe – and believe it with the same passion. They create trust, because they also give trust to others. Moreover, they demonstrate this trust not only by what they say, but primarily by what they do. It is because of this trust that they are able to motivate people to contribute towards the realization of their common vision.

Trust is the basis of every relationship. Also between leaders and followers. And there is only one right way to build trust: you have to start with yourself. Trust begins with exemplary behavior.

Unfortuantely, many leaders, organisations and institutions have a problem with 'trust'. I have noticed this in particular during my visits to Poland (although it obviously happens elsewhere). The young Polish management wolves think that the world is at their feet, just waiting for them to walk all over it. The following mail is a typical example of what I mean:

Good Morning BrunoVsky (:) xxxxxxxxx, first time our THINK TANK TEAM :)

I would like to share you experiences and thoughts after my meeting yesterday, which I had in xxxxx with the Director of Development, responsible for key projects STRATEGY in the Bank, including the merger related with xxxxxxxxxxxxxxxxxx. If we apply to this, we have a chance to work with them. We talked about several key projects for them (they are looking for partners consulting companies NOW):

1. *High Potentials in Bank: 10 years leading a project in which xxxx by choosing a group of people that have the potential to be the future managers - leaders (potential leaders today), managers in the future. But they (Bank) have a problem: these HP at the end of the program are highly excited emo-*

tionally, it seems to them that they walk 10 meters above the ground, but
from the emotional shoot a few shows. They are not suitable for managers
in the future. They cannot be the coach for the other. They have lack of emo-
tional intelligence.... I think we can help them ... moreover they should to
design new program for the NEW Bank (after mergers of Banks)

2. ....
3. ....
4. *Change - ??? any ideas for supporting...*

Bankers, even young wolves, still don't seem to have understood.

The history of Poland is one of war and conquest (rather like Belgium, in fact). This has bred mistrust and a tendency to think in terms of bosses and underlings. The older managers don't really believe in my story of a new empathic approach to leadership. And they are passing this same attitude on to the new generation of leaders. Each system creates it own values and norms, which are then translated into a form of inherited behavior. In Poland, this means that a boss is a boss – and must behave like one: expensive suit, name card, haughty demeanor, expecting respect as a right rather than something to be earned, etc. When I enter a company office in Poland, I am always met by the man in charge. This is hierarchical thinking taken to extremes. Subservience is built into their culture – in concrete. You can sense that people are deliberately holding their tongues. Yet it is totally the opposite in Polish private life. In someone's home, you are welcomed with warmth, openness, generosity and genuine interest. This makes everything possible – but not at work.

- *Why can't people work with each other in a friendly, open and respectful manner?*
- *Why do people have to lose their true self whenever they enter an office or factory?*

'Trust' has the same origins as the word 'truth'. When you give trust, you are being true to the things in which you believe: your values. These values contain the reasons that explain why you do (or don't do) a particular thing. The 'why' indicates intention, and is part of the self. The fundamental issue when assessing behavior is not therefore 'what' someone does or 'how' they do it, but rather 'why' they do it. This 'why' is inextricably linked to a person's values. The 'what' and the 'how' are simply products of this 'why', and can be influenced by all kinds of external factors.

Leaders are able to radiate their values, so that they can be picked up and adopted by others. In this way, they create a kind of collective awareness, which people can recognize, appreciate and emulate. Leaders have the power to make others believe that their cause is a good cause, a cause worth setting your own personal interests to one side for. In other words, great leaders have the ability to touch your soul, so that you choose to follow them. Not because you must, but because you want to.

Act V

The importance of values

BRONNIE WARE'S
5 biggest regrets
☑ COURAGE
☑ LESS WORK
☑ EXPRESS FEELINGS
☑ IN TOUCH W/ FRIENDS
☑ LET MYSELF be HAPPIER

MAY
↑
WANT
↑
MUST

Philadelfia LEADERSHIP 2020
NAKED TRUTH

if you die tonite...

WHAT'S YOUR INNER YOU?

CHOOSE a LIFE THAT MATTERS

?? CAN BE DONE!

X2

X2

be possibilist!

Values must be lived

Sociologist Talcott Parsons argued that all human actions are played out in four different domains. Each of these domains influences the other and they are inherently linked to each other. He claimed that each person lives in solidarity with others through a variety of economic, social, political and cultural transactions. Everything is linked to everything else, either in harmony or disharmony. Consciously or unconsciously, we make choices in life based on these four elements.

An example will make things clearer. Let us imagine that someone believes in the basic values of respect for other people, for nature and for sustainability. He (or she) builds his life around these values. He will probably give his political allegiance to a 'green' ecological party. And he will probably want to earn his living in a company that is driven by the same values as his own. At a social level, he will probably take part in local charitable or improvement projects. You get the idea? Someone working for Doctors Without Frontiers or Oxfam will look at the world from a totally different perspective than a plastic surgeon working in a private clinic in Davos. A volunteer working for an NGO in Kwazulu Natal will not look at things in the same light as a banker in the New York branch of Goldman Sachs.

Leadership begins and ends with the values that the leader puts forward and the manner in which these values are translated into exemplary behavior and practice. Leaders are judged on the basis of their 'why', the standards and norms they represent, and the manner in which they infuse these standards and norms into the DNA of their organization or movement. Because it is values, and the behavior linked to those values, that will determine whether you are prepared to believe him or not. Can you recognize yourself in his actions? Would you feel comfortable working towards his vision? Do you want to belong to the same greater whole as he does, or not?

Do his values accord with your own personal values, the ones that are buried deep in the core of your being, the ones in which you believe most passionately and are only revealed after all the outer layers of your existence have been stripped away? If so, there is a very good chance that you will support this inspirational leader in pursuit of the vision that you both share, to achieve what you both think will be a better world.

Simon Sinek's TED talk: How great leaders inspire action.

Simon Sinek, the author of *Start with Why* correctly makes a distinction between 'why', 'how' and 'what'. Everyone knows what he/she is doing and most of us know how to do it. But very few of us know why we are doing it – at least according to Sinek. Yet it is precisely that – knowing why you do something – that makes all the difference. This is the element that convinces others, this is what they buy into: not what you do, but why you do it. Inspirational leaders and inspirational organizations, irrespective of size or market segment, always think, act and communicate from inside to outside. Viewed in these terms, what you do simply proves that what you said about why you do it is true. In other words, that you truly mean what you say.

If a large group of people share the same values, this can lead to a kind of collective consciousness, a strong feeling of emotional solidarity. This strengthens the feeling of unity and solidifies the common purpose. This collective consciousness is often latent, but certain events can bring it to the surface, such as the pedophilia scandals in Belgium, or the Breivik murders in Sweden, or (in a more positive sense) the Olympic Games in London. Alternatively, look at the feeling of connectedness expressed by the victims of factory closures, whether it is Ford Genk in Belgium, or Arcelor-Mittal in France, or Philips in the Netherlands, etc., etc.

It is this collective consciousness that has the power to unite people behind a single, common thought. Leaders who can succeed in triggering this collective consciousness and can keep it actively engaged are capable of mobilizing an entire community. There are examples enough of this phenomenon in recent history, in both a positive and a negative sense.

The values of the Tea Party Movement: dangerous stuff.

At any one time, there are a large number of 'why' stories in circulation, and a large number of them are demagogic. Many are just trying to convince you that what they are offering is actually what you really want. Even if this means peddling you a bunch of lies. There is a name for this type of deception: propaganda. Why earn more money? To consume more. Why consume more? Because it is good for you and for the economy! Why send refugees back to their homeland? Because it will be one less thing to worry about! Why start a war and exterminate a whole race of people? So that there will be all the more room for us! Sounds crazy? It is – but it happens all the time.

Of course, there are values and values. The values of the Tea Party, as proclaimed in the 2012 presidential election campaign in the United States, strike me as being positively dangerous: firm action against illegal immigrants, a focus on job creation in the domestic market, a stronger army, reinforcement of the right to bear arms, the severe reduction of the state apparatus and government 'interference', the balancing of the national budget through savage welfare cuts, the lowering of taxes, an insistence on the use of English in all aspects of public life, the promotion of 'traditional' family values… Imagine that this list managed to ignite the collective consciousness in what is still the most powerful nation in the world, and imagine that this was reflected in both American national and international policy. What kind of 'project' could we expect? With what kind of end results? You don't need to be a political genius to work out the answer to that one…

Values in an organization

Whether you are talking about a company, a school, a hospital, an association or a political party, the basis for the actions of all of them are contained in their values. It is then the task of the leader to translate these values into external behavior, indicators and competencies; behavior that is visible and tangible on the work-floor. It is important to search for, or rather to feel what the values of a community are: do they really live, are they concrete and perceptible. 'What do we stand for?' 'What are the things that are fundamentally important to us?' This is the essence of the matter. So, too, is this: 'Are our professed values reflected in the way we behave?' 'Is there harmony between my values and the values of the organization I belong to?'

An organization that does not make clear what its values are, or makes this clear but does not live up to its own rhetoric, is *value*less, both literally and figuratively. In other words: worthless, good for nothing, all washed up. Many companies are guilty of this sin of omission, with all the consequences that this implies for its staff, its customers, it suppliers; in fact, for everyone involved… It is always possible to 'measure' the difference between a 'valuable' and a 'valueless' organization. Just talk with people at the bottom of the hierarchical ladder. They are the 'barometer' of an organization's trustworthiness and you will quickly get a very good idea of what is going on. After 10 minutes you will already sense whether their leaders are leading them to success or leading them to disaster.

In the business world, values are translated into skill competencies, knowledge competencies and behavioral indicators. This phenomenon is also becoming more common in schools and in the training sector. I am not in favor of this evolution. The purpose of schools is to educate our young people in a manner that is as generically and holistically complete as it is possible to be; not to draw up the competency profiles that best suit the dictates of the market and the economy. The economic activities of people are confined to just one of Talcott Parson's four dimensions; account must also be taken of the social, political and cultural dimensions. Our colleges and universities are turning out more and more operationally suitable, company-intelligent graduates. I call this partial intelligence. What does this mean? It means that you can be a brilliant surgeon, but still a complete pain-in-the-ass for everyone you work with. Or a top-class engineer, who expects all his subordinates to shut up every time he has something to say. Many surgeons and engineers are as much renowned for their smug, self-satisfied feeling of superiority as for their undoubted technical excellence. Intellectually gifted, emotionally ignorant. (Although, happily, there are exceptions, such as my good friend Professor Pedro Brugada.)

Good examples

During a congress in leadership held in Orlando (USA) in 2011, I became fascinated by the story of the CLP energy company, the main electricity supplier in India.

In response to a question about what leadership meant for CLP, the company's representative gave the following answer: *'We create a common culture; we break down the silo mentality, change it into a holistic view and create powerful leaders who generate power.'*

In other words, at CLP it is not the individual who is central, but rather the community, based on a holistic vision and founded on a common culture. The CLP model starts from the base, like the roots of a tree, which then grows upwards and outwards:

- *'What do we want to be and what message do we want to give to others as an organization?*
- *What does the leadership team do to identify itself with this cultural vision and how does it support and develop this vision for the organization?*
- *As an individual leader, how shall I find my own position within this process?*

…and, above all:

- *Can I agree with these fundamental principles?*
- *How are we going to implement these principles in a disciplined manner in all our operational teams?'*

The core values of Zappos.

In the life of an organization everything revolves around shared values: the collective consciousness. I found a good example of this on the website of Zappos.com, the online shoe and clothing company set up by Tony Hsieh and sold in 2009 for a small (or rather, a large) fortune to Amazon.com.

Here are the 10 core values of the Zappos business ethos, the message that they want to send to the world:

Deliver WOW through service.
Embrace and drive change.
Create fun and a little weirdness.
Be adventurous, creative, and open-minded.
Pursue growth and learning.
Build open and honest relationships with communication.
Build a positive team and family spirit.
Do more with less.
Be passionate and determined.
Be humble.

Why not take a look at their website page, where you can read how Zappos turns these principles into practice. Or visit the Twitter page of Tony Hsieh and click through to www.deliveringhappiness.com/about-us/. Fill in the inquiry form and discover the things that are most important to people in terms of being happy at work… Simple!

In Belgium the Federal Agency for Social Security is becoming a textbook example of an organization that seeks to create a working environment in which the happiness of the employees is paramount. There is no more clocking-in and clocking-off. The boss no longer has his own office. There is no direct supervision of staff, not even an obligation to come to work at a particular time on a particular day or number of days. Control has been replaced by good arrangements linked to good objectives through good communication. People are even allowed to work from home, if this is operationally possible.

Tony Hsieh's Twitter page.

The core values of the Federal Agency for Social Insurance are:
- *self-development*
- *solidarity*
- *trust*
- *result-orientation*
- *respect*

The agency has also created an interesting post, one of the first of its kind in Belgium: a Chief Happiness Officer. I regard this as a very daring, progressive and innovative title for the Human Resources Manager: CHO instead of HRM – great! On her LinkedIn page CHO Laurence Van Hee has written the following about her function:

'Spread happiness around you' is my philosophy.

'Freedom + Responsibility = Happiness + Performance' is my strategy.

I do not manage resources because we are not resources.
We are people. I do my best to make people happy: happy people are perform-
ing better. That's the job of a Chief Happiness Officer.

I give support to people, teams and organizations to better perform through
agile organizations, advanced workplaces (#nwow), innovative leadership
concepts 2.0 and efficient processes (EBM).

I commit as a 'resultant', advising as a consultant and achieving results meas-
urable via sustainable KPI's.

Some companies have taken matters another stage further. There are
organizations where all the employees are shareholders and the CEO earns
the same amount as an average member of staff. They have abolished the
unjustifiable differentials between the top and the bottom of the hierarchical ladder, where the big bosses were sometimes paid 20 times more
than the lowest worker and the bonuses reached levels that can reasonably be described as 'obscene'. Gone are the days of the 'grab-what-you-can'
culture. After the 'paperless company' we are now entering the era of the
'bossless company'.

Likewise, it is unbelievably stupid that people worldwide are forced to get
up at 6 o'clock every morning, stand for hours on cold platforms waiting
for trains that seldom arrive on time or spend hours in traffic jams, just so
that they can clock-on in their offices at eight-thirty on the dot, only then
to repeat the process in the opposite direction at four-thirty in the after-
noon, when they clock-off! What is the result (apart from a whole heap of
unnecessary stress)? The result is that it is often six or seven o'clock in the
evening before they arrive home. And what is the first thing they do, after
they have kissed the wife and children, and had a bite to eat? They log on
to the internet to see if there are any mails from work or to complete the
presentation they need to give next morning! And this while most of these
jobs could easily be done from home! An average of 3 hours a day in a car or
a train is equivalent to 15 hours per week. That is 60 hours a month or 660
hours a year. 82.5 working days. Per person. Multiplied by millions of people
around the world. Lost. Wasted. And why? Just so we can make sure that
people are actually working! Do you really call that 'efficient'!

Values
that can make the difference

What are the important values that we hope to see in the real leaders of the future? In my humble opinion, the following 18 values must be the pillars on which ethical and sustainable leadership is built in the years ahead:

- *Authenticity*
- *Honesty*
- *Vulnerability*
- *Humility*
- *Transparency*
- *Openness*
- *Integrity*
- *Inspiration*
- *Approachability*

- *Consistency*
- *Respect*
- *Courage*
- *Trust*
- *Love*
- *Wisdom*
- *Letting go*
- *Passion*
- *Humor*

I would like to offer a word or two of explanation about each of these values. But be careful! It is the amalgamation and interaction of all these values together that will determine whether or not your behavior is sincere.

When this happens, it is possible to talk of a synergy. 1+1=3. People only need to speak a few words with you to understand what you mean. You are automatically on the same wave length. Why? Because you radiate your values like a radio transmitter! All they need to do is pick up your signal !

AUTHENTICITY

If you stand and look at Da Vinci's *Mona Lisa* in the Louvre, you can see the enigmatic painting hanging there behind its reinforced glass panel, but it is authentic; real, not false. When you then leave the museum, you are besieged by all kinds of street-hawkers, trying to sell you copies of the great work in many different shapes and forms, all of which are obviously cheap and kitschy fakes. Authenticity is the opposite of imitation. In other words, for me an authentic leader is a leader who reveals himself to others as he really is, 'warts and all'. You know what he stands for and you know what you can expect from him.

HONESTY

There is nothing worse than a leader who lies, not only to others but also to himself. Honesty is closely related to sincerity. A real leader is sincere. He tells it as it is, even if the message is not always a pleasant one. If you want a recent example of the opposite of sincerity, look no further than Stephen Odell, the top man of Ford in Europe, who didn't have the guts to explain to the workers at Ford Genk why their factory had to close. No, instead his lordship preferred to ride in his chauffeur-driven limousine to the salons of Brussels, where he broke the news to the Belgian prime minister and the press in a terse communiqué. I can understand that there might be economic reasons for closing the factory, and I have no real problem with that (regrettable though it obviously is). Company closures are inevitable during a global crisis and multi-national corporations need to take a world-wide view. But the manner in which the staff at Ford Genk were treated was so underhand and so dishonest; it really made my blood boil! If you have something to say, then say it honestly and openly, so that people can at least understand why you have acted in a particular way. In this case, the news of the closure was read out by the director of Ford Genk from a piece of paper. And in the meantime Odell has been promoted…

VULNERABILITY

Being vulnerable means putting your emotions on the line, allowing others to see you 'in the raw', showing them 'the naked truth'. My experience with numerous leaders has taught me that those who have the courage to expose their vulnerability are also the ones who are most secure in themselves and in their position. By allowing people to see that you can feel hurt, you demonstrate that you too are a human being, not some kind of superman who is in control of every situation. This implies that you need to show genuine emotions, rather than pretending that you are made of stone. But don't take things to the opposite extreme: being vulnerable does not mean that you need to become a sentimental jerk, blubbing at the least excuse. Vulnerable leaders behave with empathy, trying to imagine and (above all) understand what the other person is feeling.

HUMILITY

Being humble means being able to admit your mistakes and being willing to put others first, rather than yourself. Someone like the Dalai Lama knows perfectly how to put this into practice, as did Gandhi and Mandela. Jean Gabin wrote a wonderful song about humility: *'Maintenant je sais, qu'on ne sait jamais…'* The more I know, the better I understand that I really know nothing. Now that's what I call humility!

TRANSPARENCY

For me, transparent leaders are leaders who follow a clear policy. Organizations run by such leaders are places of trust, rather than distrust. Places where you can look inside, so that you can see that there are no hidden agendas. Places where people feel valued and secure. Transparency means that the rules are applicable to everyone.

When Sergio Marchionne, the current CEO at Fiat, took up his job, the company was paralyzed by family disputes and union power. The value of Fiat shares on the stock exchange had hit rock bottom and the company was shaking on its very foundations. Disaster seemed imminent. Marchionne is well-known for never wearing a tie. Always a sweater. Smartly dressed, but always a sweater. Within Fiat he introduced a transparent policy. It was a 'take-it-or-leave-it' policy, but at least it was a clear policy. And what happened? People understood and accepted what was necessary. As a result, Fiat has finally got the wind back in its sails. Every employee knows what is expected of him/her and what he/she can expect in return.

You can compare many companies with a bus at night. All the employees are sitting on a seat, the curtains are closed tight and there is just a little chink of windscreen at the front, through which the driver can see. This means that the driver is the only person who knows where the bus is going; the only one who knows about the vision, the mission and the strategy. All the others are simply along for the ride. The question is: do you want to sit on this type of bus? I certainly don't! A lack of transparency has been the final nail in the coffin for many companies and organizations.

OPENNESS

No comment required: just open the door and let the world come in!

INTEGRITY

Integrity means being sincere, honest and incorruptible. People with integrity say what they mean and then do what they say. They do not fake emotions and they do not have a hidden agenda. This type of person is a blessing for any organization and for the people who work there. They live in accordance with their own norms and values, and these norms and values are found acceptable to the environment around them. This external approval is crucial. Hitler also lived in accordance with his own values and norms, but you could hardly call this evil monster a man of integrity!

INSPIRATION

To inspire others, a leader will need to do the following things: encourage, stir up, set in motion, electrify, instigate, call on, stimulate, applaud, infuse, inject, instill, suggest, impassion, urge, egg on, boost, exhort, advise, spur on, nudge, prod, rouse, foment, inflame, foster, fuel whip up, prickle, tease, push, invite, hasten, animate, improve, embolden, agitate, excite, initiate, motivate, drive on, feed, prompt, move forward, enliven, delight, vitalize, bring to the surface, evoke, call to mind, enthuse, etc., etc.

You could make an even longer list – but I am sure you get the general idea.

APPROACHABILITY

A leader who is not approachable puts too great a distance between himself and his followers. This makes it more difficult for both sides to communicate with and understand each other. This type of leader is hiding from his responsibility. The manager who works behind a closed door, who never walks around the work-floor or who seldom talks to his people cannot possibly know what is going on within his own organization. He creates an aura of inviolability and inaccessibility around his person, but is usually experienced by others as being cold and emotionless. Does this mean that a leader must be constantly present, always available to everyone? No, not really. But people must feel comfortable when they do need to approach him, and not fear that they are somehow treading on his toes or invading his private space.

CONSISTENCY

If leaders who lie are bad, leaders who are unstable and unpredictable are possibly worse. Smiling at you one day, biting your head off the next. These are leaders who take their personal moods with them each day to their work, and make their staff 'pay' for the way they are feeling. Not surprisingly, the staff quickly learn to read the barometer each morning and attune their actions to the 'mood of the day'. It is hardly the most efficient way of working, is it? Capricious leaders cause negative emotions, such as fear and insecurity: things that an organization needs like a hole in the head.

Fortunately, the personal assistant of the boss is usually able to filter the worst excesses of his/her master. The PA knows how best to deal with the daily mood swings, giving more space and more room for maneuver to others in the immediate vicinity. In short, the PA plays the role as a court jester or 'fool' in medieval times, soothing the royal temper and drawing the royal anger away from others.

RESPECT

There is nothing better than to be respected for what you have achieved as a person, a manager or a leader. Respect means being open to other ideas, other beliefs, other attitudes. Diversity and multi-culturalism are an enrichment, not an impoverishment. Transglobal thinking is great, once you have tried it. Respect also means that your behavior is very empathic. But you must remember that respect does not come automatically and you cannot force someone to give it to you. No, it needs to be earned. Many managers seem to believe that a dominant, authoritative approach is enough to gain the respect of their staff. This is the old 'doctor-lawyer-bank manager' syndrome of the past, when certain people were respected simply because of the position they held in society. My father portrayed this brilliantly in the Belgian film *Het gezin van Paemel*, a story about the demise of a farming family at the hands of the local gentry. Watching it still gives me goosebumps. Bravo, Senne.

Some high-born families still find it acceptable to express the narcissistic sentiments of what they see as their own inborn superiority. They look down on ordinary folk with arrogance and disdain, living in the cold rooms of their castles, still served by lackeys and flunkies. They are no longer in touch with the real world, but still wish to perpetuate their caste through inbreeding and inter-marriage with 'the right people'. Fortunately, people who have acquired certain positions simply because of their birth – the lords and ladies of yesteryear – are no longer able to dictate to the rest of us, in the manner that Baron de Wilde was able to dictate to Farmer van Paemel. Nowadays, the aristocracy have to earn their respect – just like everyone else. And that is only right and proper.

COURAGE

Daring, bravery, guts: yes, leaders, like athletes and soldiers, need to have a good dose of courage and perseverance to achieve their objectives. Leaders without objectives, leaders without a vision, leaders who avoid tensions or buck the hard decisions: those are not leaders, they are just wimps in disguise. Men and women who want to be leaders must have the courage of their convictions, must be prepared to defend their opinions publicly, but without enforcing them on others. No guts no glory!

TRUST

This is one of the most important virtues, since it is the basis for all stable relationships between people. It is often the product of a combination of different factors, but one thing is certain: the development of trust must always begin with yourself. You must first believe in your own person before you can believe in others. And once you have achieved this, you must first give your trust to others, before you can expect to get trust back from them in return.

LOVE

Makes the world go around. Do you need a picture?

WISDOM

Wisdom leads to humility. By wisdom I do not mean the technical ability to run a company or organization. No, wisdom in this context is generally to be found in those leaders who are prepared to ask questions, instead of assuming that they already know all the answers. Leadership blindness (or stupidity, if you prefer) can only lead to disaster. What do I mean by 'blindness'? Believing that your version of the truth is the only possible version of that truth. You would be amazed how often this happens.

LETTING GO

Daring to let go means giving people the freedom to express themselves and take responsibility for their own actions. The word 'autonomy' is derived from the Greek words *autos,* meaning 'the self', and *nomos,* meaning 'rules'. Someone who works autonomously therefore rules themselves, without the need for a boss to be looking over their shoulder all the time, to make sure that the work is being done 'properly'. If you are prepared to let go in this manner, it is still important to make clear arrangements about the 'how' and the 'why'. The only thing as a leader that you then still need to control is the 'what': the end result.

So let your people go! Set them free to do their own thing! If the rules of their freedom are clearly defined and there is full transparency about the objectives they are expected to achieve, most people are more than happy to go along with this method of working It's a bit like driving a car. There are a certain number of traffic rules that you are expected to obey. You are free to comply with these rules or to ignore them completely – it's up to you. But you know that if you get behind the wheel when you are drunk, you form not only a risk to yourself but also to others – and consequently may have to accept some serious consequences for your actions. My children have been biking to school for years, and we also let them visit their friends by bus and train. Why? Because I think you cannot keep on pampering your children for ever; otherwise they will never grow up. They have to learn to stand on their own two feet. And it is the same in companies and organizations. People will never maximize their full potential unless you let them show what they are capable of.

PASSION

Passion in this context relates to effort, drive, determination, giving it 110%, etc. If you let your staff talk about their hobbies, you will notice how their faces immediately light up with excitement. Leaders with passion are the same: they always give it their best shot. Once again, however, it is not necessary to go to extremes. There must be commitment, but it does not need to be to the exclusion of everything else. I see many leaders who expect their staff to work as hard as they do. But hard work is not the same as passion. On the contrary, hard work is often just a means to run away from something: partner, family, friends, trouble, responsibility… When these people get old and retire, they suddenly find that they have no real life and their world collapses. Many of them don't even reach pension age.

I prefer to opt for a passionate life, rather than a life of late trains, traffic jams, stress and mind-numbing routine. I like what I do and I have to work hard to make a success of it. But I do it with plenty of passion, plenty of humor, plenty of play – and lots and lots of happiness.

HUMOR

It is often said that people who laugh a lot live longer than people who are always miserable. I can believe it! I also believe that leaders with a sense of humor are better able to engage people that leaders with a heart of stone (and a face to match). Humor allows us to put things in perspective. Making people laugh means making them happy. And that can't be bad, can it? Not only is it not bad, it is also efficient. Happy people work harder, so that organizational performance improves. In other words, funny people are worth their weight in gold, since they generate energy in others.

Leaders who are unhappy – and do nothing about it – are a curse for their staff. People without humor poison the atmosphere for everyone. You can almost see the bad temper oozing out of them. Their cynicism and sarcasm can rot an organization from within. Give me a fun group with chaotic, half crazy people, who just enjoy being alive!

Values must live

Values must live. Values that are just framed on a wall, gathering dust, are of no use to anyone. In many organizations the core values are decided at the top and then printed out on expensive-looking paper, before being passed on to the rest of the staff, like Moses handing down the Ten Commandments. 'Look, this is what we want to be! This is what we want you to be!' 'Yeah, right, sure,' you can hear the not-all-that-impressed staff reply. You might just as well hang one of those fake Mona Lisa's on your foyer wall. It would be just as phony, but at least it has the virtue of being decorative! No, in this way you will never achieve anything. Values need to be translated into implicit modes of behavior: patterns of action taken by the organization in which the core values will shine through. Drawing up a list of the right values for your organization is never a simple task, but you can make it easier by asking the people who already know: your staff! Ask them what kind of organization they want to work in and what kind of behavior this entails. You may need to adjust this list slightly to reflect the realities of your business situation, but in these circumstances the values that you hang in your fancy frame in your nice foyer will at least be real values, values that are widely held and appreciated by your employees.

Whenever I enter the office of a new CEO at the start of a new assignment, I always make it a point to read the core values hanging on his wall. I then ask the CEO if I can borrow them for a while. The majority show surprise. Many of them even ask: 'What on earth for?!' 'Well,' I explain, 'I am going to take these values down to the work-floor and see if they are actually real, authentic and lived.' This is the point when the CEO usually breaks out into a cold sweat... So now you know: when you hire me to do a satisfaction and motivation survey, it won't cost you a fortune. I'll just pop down to the work-floor and ask the people what is good about the organization and what can still be improved. And when I give leadership seminars in badly-run companies, I still hear the same question over and over again. 'Bruno that's all well and good, and we really do believe in these values, honestly,... but could you maybe say that to those people upstairs, because they don't seem to understand...' (sic)

Happiness on the work-floor

The list of an organization's values is always interesting. Moreover, it is always easy to assess values. There is only one criterion you need to apply:

- *Will the roll out of these values result in increased happiness?*

The search for happiness has never been so intense as it is now. The need for happiness is universal. What's more, happiness is not something that you should only find away from your place of work. First work your socks off between 9 and 5, only then to be happy during the evenings and at weekends? No, that's not the way it's supposed to work. And it's certainly not how the young people of today look at things. They are not prepared to live the same 'fragmented' lives as their parents and grandparents. They want to be happy both at work and outside – and not just outside. As these young people get older and make careers for themselves, so this desire will become more entrenched at the higher levels of companies and organizations.

100 happiness professors and professional specialists from 50 countries talk about the search for happiness and what it means.

Happiness at work should be possible. Must be possible. Is possible. And that implies friendship. In other words, there must be a place for friendly leadership.

Leo Bormans has written an excellent book on 'happiness', with usable advice gathered from a hundred experts from all around the planet; advice based on years of valid scientific research. Herman Van Rompuy, the European president, sent Bormans' *The World Book of Happiness* as a New Year's gift to the leader of every country in the world. This just highlights the importance that is now being given, in both political and academic circles, to this crucial subject. And the good news is that a *World Book of Love* is also in the pipeline.

Manfred Kets de Vries on happiness.

In another book about happiness, Manfred Kets de Vries refers to three important prerequisites for achieving it: you need something to do, something to strive for and have people around you who love you. Self-knowledge and the pursuit of happiness are inextricably linked with each other: if you lack the first, the second is doomed to failure. It's as simple as that. No management theory is necessary. Just common sense…

I believe that the search for happiness can create a new balance in all different kinds of organization: political, social, cultural and economic. A move from dehumanization to humanization.

Why do you think that so many satisfaction and motivation studies are carried out in the business world? The essence of these studies is to establish whether or not people feel happy in what they do. However, they are often misused in an attempt to show that staff are happy, satisfied and well-motivated – even when they are not. Because the happiness of many people at work must be open to question. If everyone is so happy, why are stress and burn-out at an all-time high? If people are being bullied or are forced to work long hours in such difficult conditions that some of them actually prefer the terrible alternative of suicide (such as has recently happened at France Telecom and Foxconn), then clearly there is still a lot wrong with our work ethic.

Act VI

Quick wins

POLITICAL
LEADERSHIP

♂  ♀ DEMOGRAPHY

ⲧⲏⲉ **5** GENERATIONS
BOBOS-...COCOS--
-->MOMOS-YOYOS Ⴘ

REVOLUTION #OCCUPY...

GLOCALISATION

TSUNAMIS

Connectivity...

Tsunami-alarm

'You say you want a revolution… Well you know, we all want to change the world.' So sang John Lennon back in the 1960s. Sometimes it is possible to pin-point specific moments in history when mankind turned a corner and starting moving in a different direction. The invention of the wheel was just such a moment. So too was the discovery of penicillin or the first use of oil as a source of energy. Of course, there have also been negative turning points, such as the election of Adolf Hitler as chancellor of Germany in 1933. All landmark moments, each revolutionary in its own different way. The past is littered with them.

Some revolutions creep up on us slowly and silently, like a virus infecting your body and destroying it from within, deadly before you even realize its danger. In contrast, other revolutions allow us to gradually evolve towards a better society.

I would like to take you through a series of revolutions that in my opinion will strongly influence the way we live and work in the decades ahead. It is even possible to speak of a tsunami, because that is how great their impact will be.

If we do not prepare properly for the arrival of this tsunami and adjust our style of leadership accordingly to meet its challenges, society may take a huge step backwards in its evolution. In particular, our Western way of life will be shaken to its very foundations, at every social level.

Hans Rosling subjects demographic statistics to his own unique kind of analysis. Only by increasing the standard of living of the very poorest will it be possible to stop the growth of the world's population.

I will not be talking about great macro events, such as global warming, demographic change, the growing power of the Asian Tiger economies, the exhaustion of fossil fuels, our hunger for energy, the rise of new capitalism and the green economy.

Of course, this does not mean that these challenges are not equally as serious, nor that we do not need to find urgent answers to the problems that they pose. On the contrary. And once again, a new kind of leadership will be required.

But I fear that the old style of leadership will not come up with the necessary solutions in time. The dark clouds that have been blown up by 'the system' are thick and difficult to penetrate.

Paul Collier wrote a brilliant book about the impact of poor leadership on poverty and war in Africa.

In recent decades a wide range of different systems and structures have been designed, each with the intention of giving new direction to our society. This has resulted in the creation of a worldwide apparatus, with different steps, levels and links. Every step, level or link has its own position in the pecking order, so that some are more important than others. Each of these structures is manned by people. Sometimes they are chosen on the basis of merit, sometimes for the purpose of defending the vested interests of those with power. All the structures are fed by study bureaus, lobby workers, interest groups, political parties, people with authority and prestige. They consume statistics, research results and jargon at an amazing rate; they digest opinions, arguments and points of view; and they excrete rules, laws, conventions and vetoes that confirm their own position and power.

Structures often reflect the balance of power at the time of their creation. Once they have been set up, their objective is to maintain that balance of power. Even though the external realities of the world outside might have changed. Structures are always interested in self-preservation and for this reason it is expected that they will defend the special concerns of their sponsors and supporters. In exchange, they receive a share of the authority and prestige referred to above. Their activities are focused on one specific aim: to acquire more for their own group than any other group and, once they have acquired it, to hold on to it.

As long as there is growth, so that the economic 'cake' is large enough to give everyone a decent share, there is no problem. However, once there is economic shrinkage, so that the situation soon degenerates into a stalemate. Sometimes decisions are taken to do 'something', sometimes decisions are taken to do nothing, sometimes decisions are taken to decide later. Change and innovation become difficult, because change and innovation risk affecting the vested interests. It becomes even more difficult when it is necessary to re-think an entire system or way of life. But that is precisely what we need to do at the present time.
Changing a system can best be done from the inside out.

In this chapter we will be looking primarily at shocks at micro level; the shocks that every leader can expect to be confronted with in the near future; the shocks that they can actually do something positive about. We can call these shocks a series of 'quick wins'. The realization of these quick wins will help to adjust the system from within, making it better prepared to cope with the larger macro shocks that are unquestionably on their way.

First, however, I need to correct something I said earlier. We will, in fact, be looking at demographic evolutions. Not with lots of facts and figures (you can find these via the QR code in the margin), but in terms of their effect on organizations and the leaders of tomorrow. After all, demographics are about people – and so is leadership.

The demographic future of Europe and the challenges it presents.

More old people – but of a different kind

In Europe more and more people are surviving to pensionable age. It is esti-mated that by 2050 one in ten Europeans will be older than 80 years old. What's more, the birth rate is not high enough to maintain existing popula-tion levels. It is the same story in Japan, which is ageing even faster than Europe, with depopulation as a result. In China the 'one-child' policy imple-mented since the 1960s has created a surplus of men. Societies that are getting progressively older are faced with an almost impossible challenge: how can they continue to fund the social safety-net for the old and infirm, if fewer and fewer young people are joining the labor market and paying tax?

On the reverse side of the coin, it must be remembered, of course, that some societies do not have the same 'good fortune' of ageing. Average life expectancy in South Africa, for example, is around 50 years of age.

In countries where the population is ageing, organizations are ageing as well. This is something new. Until now, organizations have been accustomed to recruiting young, new talent and getting rid of their old fuddy-duddies. They have been able to renew, almost constantly. From now on, this will no longer be possible. It will not be acceptable to send older employees on pre-retirement schemes, simply because society will not be able to avoid it. Moreover, young talent will become harder and harder to find, so it will not always be easy to replace 'outgoing' talent, no matter how old it is.

This means that organizations in ageing countries need to develop a radi-cal new approach towards their ageing workforce. In Belgium, for example, you are now officially regarded as an 'elderly employee' if you are past the age of 50. In other words, you are winding down to your pension, so that there is no point in 'wasting' further resources on your talent. As a result, you are given very few opportunities (if any) on the job market, because people (or rather managers) think that 'oldies' are expensive, set in their ways, difficult to train, and unable to deal with modern systems and pro-cesses. In other words, today's short-sighted corporate business model says that it makes better economic sense to write off this group of workers than to invest in them.

All older people are tarred with the same brush. But that is an easy option – and a wrong one, too. In the future more and more organizations will be happy to try and keep their older talent on board. Because companies face a challenge every bit as serious as the societal challenge I mentioned earlier: how can they prevent their capital – their human talent – from becoming disastrously watered down? There is a very real risk of a new 'brain drain': the exodus of older employees, with all the knowledge and skills they possess.

HOW CAN WE ENSURE THAT OLDER EMPLOYEES REMAIN AT WORK LONGER?

It is necessary to define new boundaries. At the present time, organizations ditch older members of staff in huge numbers. A quick bit of restructuring and suddenly hundreds (if not thousands) of 50-plussers find themselves on a compulsory pre-retirement scheme. (It is striking to note that employers are against this practice at macro level, but are all to willing to use it at micro level!) On the other side of the coin, older workers are often happy to take this opportunity to step out of the labour market prematurely. Many of them feel drained, unable to cope with the pressure of new systems and/or increasingly-demanding bosses. In short, they have had enough. This can apply to older leaders, too: exhausted, overstressed, mentally and spiritually empty. Why not get out while the going is good, before they have a heart-attack or a stroke? And this is precisely what many of them do, at the earliest possible opportunity (I mean get out, not have a heart attack…).

Unfortunately, it is the impression created by these 'burnt-out cases' that determines the image of older employees in general. This is unfair and illogical. There are huge differences between people in the same age group. It is ridiculous to regard them all in the same light. There will always be those who cannot wait for pre-retirement (often justifiably), but there will also be those who want to (and are able to) carry on working until they are 80!

We all know that we will have to work longer in the future, in order to keep our social services functioning. And if there are people who still find it fun to be in active employment after the age of 50, 60 or even 70, then they should be encouraged to stay on. In this way, it might finally be possible to change the current pension mentality, with all its potential problems for the years ahead.

WHY DON'T ORGANIZATIONS ALTER THEIR WORK CULTURE BY ENCOURAGING OLDER EMPLOYEES TO STAY IN SERVICE LONGER?

Being a good leader in a company means that you need to ensure the happiness of <u>all</u> the employees, even if they have passed their 50th birthday. This in turn means that you need to communicate openly and develop alternative work arrangements, which are better suited to the needs of the more mature worker. This implies continuing to invest in their retraining, perhaps on more than one occasion. It also implies the need to organize high-quality part-time work with maximum flexibility. In short, you must show them new opportunities instead of showing them the door. To make this possible, demotion must become a discussable subject, so that hopefully a more positive culture can be created around this sensitive issue. It is also important that the older employees should be treated like everyone else and that they should continue to be actively involved in team activities. This might mean pairing a younger member of staff with an older person, who can then act in a coaching or mentoring role (if he/she has the necessary competencies). Elderly employees must not be regarded as a single homogenous group; you always need to look at the individual behind that wrinkled old face!

When older employees start talking about pre-retirement, it is usually a sign that they would like more time to do 'other things' and that they would prefer to choose their own working hours, in order to give them the added 'freedom' their desire. Good leaders must know and understand how this work/non-work balance looks from the perspective of their 50-plussers. It also means that within the framework of this balance you must still give them further opportunities to develop their value to the organization in the best possible manner. Does this involve giving them greater individual care and attention? Yes, it does – but nowadays there are HR computer programs that can easily deal with these matters.

It should also be remembered that many people past the formal retirement age are keen to carry on working. Once again, there are no ready-made solutions, but each company has tasks that older people may enjoy carrying out. So why not build a job (part-time or otherwise) around these tasks?

Fewer young people – but also of a different kind

A statistic: between now and 2050 the total population in Europe will fall by an estimated 50 million people. In most European countries, the number of young people is already declining. This means that from now on we can expect a general shortage in labor market and the number of acute shortage professions will increase. More and more older people will retire and there just won't be enough youngsters to fill the resulting vacancies. For many organizations this poses a real threat.

The knowledge that in the near future large numbers of older employees will be leaving companies means that securing a steady influx of new young talent has become a crucial factor in the business world and in society at large. Here, too, leaders must show inventive and inspiring leadership, if we hope to deal with the situation satisfactorily.

As a result, leadership in our schools, worldwide, will also play a key role in the development of our young people, our future leaders in the making. But this does not happen in the same manner everywhere. There are differences that can lead to problems.

The role of schools in the development of good leadership.

This shortage of talent obviously means that the job-seekers are in a strong position. In the coming decades, every company will be fishing in the same rapidly shrinking pool, so that the talented youngsters still swimming around in this pool will be more or less able to pick and choose their jobs. In these circumstances, it seems likely that the youngsters will opt for the organizations that show respect for their values and the way they want to live their lives. Companies that still adopt an old-fashioned, paternalistic style of leadership can expect to lose out in this battle for new talent – and will probably also lose most of the existing talent they already have.

- *How can your leadership style help you to project a 'sexy' image as an employer?*

- *How can you make your work environment attractive for the coming generations?*

In most companies the top positions are manned by the 'old brigade' with the 'young lions' occupying positions in middle management or on the lower rungs of the ladder. This age pyramid encourages a traditional, conservative style of management, based on standard formulas, processes and procedures. The message seems to be: 'No change please!' However, young people look at work in a different way than the older generation. Consequently, they expect a different type of leadership as well: they demand respect, trust and opportunities for self-development. In short, they want to strike a balance in their existence, in their 'being'. Work must be a meaningful part of this balance, but no more than that: just a part, not the be-all and end-all of everything, as was so often the case in the past. For the youth of today, there is no longer the same clear distinction between work and private life as there was in days gone by. Nowadays, these two elements need to be blended harmoniously. Young people want to work to live, not live to work.

The 2020 workplace by Jeanne Meister & Karie Willyerd

Most of the older leaders have difficulty understanding and accepting these demands. This results in a clash in leadership, between the old guard, who still expect the youngsters to work as hard and as long as they did, and the younger generation of managers, who try to divide their time more evenly between their different lives as a person. The 'oldies' have worked all their professional careers to create material prosperity for society as a whole, but they are now seeing all their efforts destroyed by a crisis of gigantic proportions, while all the young 'whippersnappers' can say is: 'Fuck the system; we want to live, and live differently!' What's more, this has nothing to do with being 'green'; you can find the same demands in the youth movements of nearly every political party.

Therefore, the differences are huge. The youngsters already regarded e-mail as outdated. They now communicate with each other via a mixture of social media platforms, such as Skype, Twitter and Facebook. (The latter still allows you to send faxes, or rather allows the fax machine to be served by your electronic 'secretary'!). Just imagine (if you can) what the world will be like for the following generation: the millennium generation. From the cradle onwards, they will grow up with 24/7 exposure to social media, smart phones, 4G, 5G and probably even 6G networks.

I am 57 years old and am privileged to have two lovely daughters, aged 15 and 17 years, who are right in the middle of this new generation. I ask them if they are ready to come and eat by SMS. 'Leadership at a distance', I call it. There is no point in just shouting up the stairs, since I know they will both be wearing headphones. I would have more success with a carrier pigeon or a message in a bottle! When they eventually arrive at table, the battle begins to try and get them to put their smart phones to one side for just 5 minutes! However, 5 minutes is a long time when you are 15 and 17! Between the starter and the main course, they have both probably received 20 to 25 SMS's, tweets, Facebook updates, etc., etc. This is the moment for a strategic 'I've just got to go to the toilet', followed by the pre-programmed behavior of every young person whenever they leave a room: pick up the smart phone and check your messages. Give them a waterproof smart phone and they would even text each other in the shower! The modern generation does not communicate with its tongue, but with its thumbs! What would Darwin make of all this? We already know that the hands of a painter, pianist or violinist can physically change as a result of their profession. So what will the hands of our young people be like in 50 years time? The speed with which their digits move over the virtual keyboard is amazing. I get stressed just watching them!

The positive aspect of this story is that the younger generation is far better connected with the world than in the past. Nowadays, there is no such thing as 'far away'; everything is relatively close (at your fingertips, in fact). They are constantly being updated about what is happening, where it is happening and why it is happening, via Facebook (my children have between 1,200 and 1,500 friends), Twitter pages, game consoles or one of the dozens of automatic news sites that now exist. No wonder we are talking more and more about 'glocalisation kids'!

A fun film about the Y Generation? Watch Greg Justice on Youtube.

Many members of the older generation think that the word 'friend' is wrongly used in this context. I don't agree. For young people their online contacts are precisely that: friends. Okay, some of them are closer friends than others, but they all exchange messages, share common interests, etc. What is that if not a form of friendship? Moreover, these new friends are spread all over the world (or at least my daughters' friends are) and can all be contacted with the same message at the touch of a single key. In the past, if you wanted to contact your loved ones abroad, you had to write (yes, actually write!) a letter on flimsy air-mail paper – and then wait up to 14 days for an answer (or six weeks if your sweetheart was in America). Now you don't even have to wait 14 seconds for an answer! Like most developments, instant communication has its advantages and disadvantages. It is a learning process that we all will have to get used to – because it is here to stay.

The Z Generation was born with the internet and has watched social media grow and grow; the Y Generation has grown with it and into it.
It is a generation distinguished by the following characteristics:

- *They live with technology.*
- *They regard the world as a flat place without boundaries.*
- *They are performance-driven.*
- *They like to work in hubs.*
- *They are mission-focused.*
- *They want more than one career pathway.*
- *They are multi-taskers and multi-learners.*
- *They share large amounts of information with their communities.*
- *They speak their own language.*
- *They use their own tools.*
- *They want to be happy both inside and outside work.*

These characteristics have led them to demand new values and a new type of behavior in their work environment. Future leaders would be wise to take account of these demands. So would our existing, older leaders. Otherwise, they might find that all their talented birds have flown.

- *How can you best communicate with this new group of young people?*

You need to alter your communication tools to reflect the usage of young people. It is impossible to do it the other way around. This means that you need to create social media sites within your company. Build your own community. Get on Twitter and Flickr. Make a company Facebook page. Give the task of managing and updating these tools to a young person, someone who knows the media and how to use them. Also give them the freedom to make instant decisions and take instant action, when they feel this is necessary. Make clear agreements with them about what is allowed and what is forbidden. Do this on the basis of a clear understanding of the values for which the company stands. To begin with, check regularly to ensure that these agreements/values are being respected.

The use of social media allows you to keep the distance between your organization and young people to a minimum. Too many companies and their leaders regard social media as a wrong use of time for their employ-ees. But the youth of today lives with and in social media. For them, it is interconnected with everything they do – including work.

In the music business, which has suffered more than most as a result of the internet, many artists and bands have understood the significance of the new trends. Internet allows you told build up more new relation-ships, but they are more superficial than in the past. Today you can be a fan of A, B and C, irrespective of whether they are soul, rock or country. You can no longer be pigeon-holed – or pilloried –by the way you dress! These developments also make it possible for mega-stars to build up online rela-tionships with their fans. Justin Bieber, Lady Gaga and many others all have their own community. And whoever joins the com-munity enjoys special privileges. In this manner the 'visible' record companies have nearly all gone virtual. As have our banks (ING has already made good progress, so too have Virgin, Keytrade, etc.). However, banks find it more difficult to attract fans and friends (certainly after the events of the last decade), and there is no guarantee that the banks of today will be acceptable as the banks of tomorrow for the younger generation.

A clever YouTube film about the power of social media: Social Media Revolution 2011.

If organizations fail to jump on the social media bandwagon, they will soon find a huge gulf opening up between them and the under-30s. Companies such as Starbucks, SAP, Trader Joe, Harley Davidson and many others have understood this truth and have appointed a Social Media Officer, or even created a separate Social Media Department.

Furthermore, in the future every organization will not only need a CEO but also a CMO: a Chief Media Officer. It is vital that the person filling this post is young: they must be able to understand the attitudes and language of Generation Y! But who is in charge of the marketing department in most companies? Exactly. A baby-boomer, or someone from the Generation X or even a dyed-in-the-wool traditionalist. And they are all illiterate when it comes to modern social media.

- *So why not appoint a young Chief Media Officer?*

It is necessary here to make an important distinction. We are not talking about social *media*, but about *social* media. It is not about projecting one-sided marketing messages, but about building up relationships, about set-ting up a community with all your stakeholders.

Consequently, it is vital that leaders and their organizations should start thinking in terms of these 'communities', rather than in terms of market 'segments'. Their focus must become people-oriented instead of commerce-oriented. Networking must take the place of channeling. Social chaos must take the place of process control and hierarchy.

The worldwide social media storm is currently at its height and still has a long way to go before it subsides. I am certain that there are still many leaders who believe that everything will essentially stay the same as in the past. I believe that they are wrong. I can see a transformation coming, a huge transformation that will have a serious impact on:

- content
- control
- place
- time
- power

When will it happen? Sooner than you think. In fact, much sooner than you think! It will happen silently, but it will happen – and there is nothing we can do to stop it. I am convinced that we are evolving towards a more 'open' form of society; a back-to-basics return to the days of tribes, in which everyone and everything is linked in an open atmosphere, and where social organization is based on communities rather than on states or markets; communities in which everything is shared and everyone commits to production for the benefit of the community as a whole, and where everyone trusts each other and there is no need of command-and-control procedures to keep everyone in check.

The P2P Foundation and Michel Bauwens.

Michel Bauwens and his colleagues at the P2P Foundation have conducted interesting peer-to-peer research on this subject. Michel is regarded as one of the '100 Most Enriching People' on the planet. The P2P Foundation follows and analyzes all peer-to-peer developments. Their work covers a number of diverse domains, from knowledge (Wikipedia, Wikileaks, etc.) through software (Linux, Open Office, etc) to production (Wikispead, Arduino, etc.). The different initiatives are monitored and charted, and their characteristics are inventoried. The

Watch his TED speeches.

conclusions reached by these investigations suggest that a paradigm shift for organizations and companies is just around the corner, a shift that will provide new and alternative forms to replace the existing organizational and collaborative models.

More young people – of yet another different kind

A wrong title? No, not at all. In some countries there will indeed be more young people in the years ahead. For example, the population in Turkey is set to grow by 20% between now and the year 2030. A number of countries already have a surplus of young people. Not because more of them are being born, but because of the crisis. And all these young people, wherever they may be, will also want their share of the global cake.

If we in Europe are likely to be faced with shortages in the labor market, immigration might seem like an obvious solution to the problem. It seems certain the call for 'foreign' talent will increase.

The population pyramid in Europe has already been supported by similar waves of immigration in the past. Was this not the case, overall population levels in the continent would have begun shrinking even sooner. I know it is an oversimplification, but if you were to remove all the immigrants in Europe from the scenario, we would already be in the middle of a major ageing crisis. Likewise, if you were to discount active economic immigration, our social security and welfare systems would already be in a state of collapse. Those who argue that a blanket ban of further immigration will work in Europe's favor are clearly barking up the wrong tree. In the years ahead we will actually need more immigration, not less: to take care of our old people and to fill all the work vacancies that would otherwise remain open. In short, we need a repetition of the 1950s and 1960s, when first the Italians and later the Moroccans and Turks came to take on the jobs that nobody else wanted.

European youth is being hard hit by the crisis. Viola Caon left Italy to find work. She has now returned to see how her former classmates are getting on. Greek and Spanish youngsters were also interviewed.

It is open to question, of course, whether or not the West will still seem like the Promised Land to the peoples of other continents.

The new waves of emigration and immigration are already in movement, primarily as a result of the economic crisis, which has hit the countries of southern Europe particularly hard, with huge levels of unemployment as a result. The young people of our continent have never been under such great pressure before. Many young Spaniards are now turning their back on their own country to seek fame and fortune (or at least a job) in the new growth economies of Latin America. Tens of thousands are leaving each year – and their decision is easy to understand. More than 50% of the under-24s in Spain are out of work. Some have even made their way to Belgium, usually to take up jobs in one of the shortage professions, such as nursing (in the care sector) or engineering (in the building sector). The same is true of Generation Y in Portugal. Like the majority of the Spaniards, their Promised Land is no longer to be found in Europe, but in the Portuguese ex-colony of Brazil. In Italy a quarter of all young people are also unemployed. Competition is fierce even to get an unpaid training post or a poorly paid (and often dangerous) manual job. In Greece it is even worse with 34% of the under-24s on state welfare. Many of them are leaving Athens to return to the islands and the countryside, where at least they can fish, farm or care for elderly members of their family. Similarly, many young Belgians of Turkish origin are returning to Turkey, where economic growth figures are still positive rather than negative. And besides, there at least they are treated as a person, and not as a 'Turk'…

Cultural shifts

As a consequence of ageing and immigration, the population mix in Western countries is destined to changed significantly in the decades ahead. This new reality is already making itself evident in urban environments, but soon its effects will also be felt in the countryside.

The transcontinental movement of population groups, with the attendant problems of cultural and religious integration (or conflict?), will de facto have a huge impact on society, both at local, national and international level. Waves of immigration are inevitably accompanied by 'cultural importation', so that peoples in the West will need to become accustomed to and reconciled with different values, customs, norms, religious beliefs, social constructions, etc. These can all have a knock-on effect – both positive and negative – at economic, political and societal level.

Some examples? Just look at the impact of the international community in Brussels, the Muslim communities in Brussels, Antwerp and Ghent (Belgium), the Indian community in Durban (South Africa), or the Chinese community in Cape Town (also South Africa). Yet more dramatic in its consequences is the spread of the Taliban throughout Afghanistan and Pakistan. Even the United States is not immune. Its population is becoming more Hispanic with each passing year, a factor of significance in the recent presidential election of 2012. Will the Democrats and Republicans still be the only political parties in the year 2050? Can they continue to represent all the ideals of all America's different ethnic groups? I doubt it. It is a similar tale in South Africa, where a growing group of literate, middle class, black citizens are having a huge influence on housing construction, the economy and even the food chain (with manioc and potatoes giving way to healthier vegetables and better meat). At a slightly different level, a competition to select the best chip shop in Limburg (a province of Belgium) was recently won by Ming Chen and Benny Wu of Lommel. If a Chinese couple can make the best chips in Belgium, the land that invented the chip and where chips are an integral part of the national culture, then anything is possible. Believe me, we ain't seen nothing yet!

The changes that will affect our societies in the coming decades are certain to be far-reaching, even dramatic. To survive as a leader in the new environments of tomorrow, it will be necessary to adopt a creative approach to cultural diversity. Leadership must inevitably become multi-cultural. The question is whether our older leaders will be able to adapt to this changing situation. Let us hope so, because multi-cultural communities also can generate positive forces – as anyone who has ever visited New York will tell you.

True, the black community in the Big Apple still has a number of issues to resolve, but in general there is an intermixing of different races, which results in great vibrancy. You can find cultures from every corner of the world, but they all seem to merge and flow into each other in a fairly homogenous manner, creating a bubbling, lively and fascinating city of some 10 million souls, which is also one of the safest metropolitan areas in the United States. Which, sadly, is something that cannot be said for Brussels…

If New York can do it, why can't Brussels? Why?

New York is highly cosmopolitan, a melting pot of different races. Like the 'cosmopolitan chicken project' of artist Koen Van Mechelen. Let's create Golems all over the world! Thanks Koen!

Five generations on the work-floor

In the near future, five different generations will be employed on the work-floor. Working together. This has never happened before in the history of mankind. How are we going to make it a success? How are the oldest and the youngest going to collaborate?

The so-called 'war on talent', combined with a growing lack of young people and a growing lack of respect shown by many of the older leaders, will soon force us to our knees, so that we will have to search for a new style of leadership. A style of leadership that will need to give new shape and form to the concept of 'living and working together', with the emphasis being placed firmly on the 'together' element of the equation.

The working population is ageing. If people in future retire from work at a later age (as seems inevitable), the youngsters will soon find themselves confronted with more and more 'oldies' (golden or otherwise) on the work-floor. With older leaders, too. This evolution will lead to a startling development: in the near future, for the first time in history, five different generations will be employed on the work-floor:

- *the traditionalists or veterans of the post-war generation :aged 60 plus*
- *the baby-boomers : currently aged 40 to 60 years*
- *the X generation :currently aged 30 to 40 years*
- *the Y generation: currently aged 20 to 30 years*
- *the millennials : currently aged 20 years or younger*

In the marketing literature you can find plenty of information about the differences and similarities between the various generations. Some of the terminology used is quite good fun: the coco's (60+), the bobo's (40-60), the momo's (30-40) and the yoyo's (15-30), although it is difficult to regard this last group as a generation. They all have different values, enjoy different interests, have different needs and different ideas about what to expect from a leader. The problem is not so much one of a difference in ages, but rather a lack of understanding about each other's patterns of expectation. People from different generations just don't know enough about each other. We find hard to imagine what each other's lives are like, and that makes it more difficult to converse with each other and (more importantly) work together.

But don't despair! There is hope! It is possible to learn about each other's pattern of expectations. You can even do it in a playful manner. During a workshop for a large international company we used all kinds of goodies and gadgets to represent the different generations: clothes, lp's, books, toys, walkmans, travel guides, magazines, computers from the 1980s... We found something that was perfect for every age group; sometimes in a flea market, sometimes in our cellar at home, sometimes in a trendy store. Using each object as a starting point, we focused on the memories that the objects evoked for each generation. And once the memories started to come to the surface, so too did information about each generation's desires and interests. It soon became clear that, as people, we all share a number of common desires and interests, irrespective of age. By talking openly with each other about these desires and interests, you create a bond, as well as respect and even a degree of affection.

This is a crucial point. It is easy (and necessary) to analyze the differences between the generations. It is more difficult (but equally necessary) to assess the factors that bind the different generations together. In our inter-generational workshops we always explain the former, but we place the emphasis squarely on the latter. What unites is always more important than what divides...

Age is just one of many different parameters. No matter how old you are – young, ancient or somewhere in between – we all have the same primeval values. It is simply that these values are given different expression in our different mode of behavior.

An example. Everyone wants to be respected. For an older person, this might mean being addressed as Mr. or Mrs., or Sir or Madam. Whereas younger people would prefer to be addressed with a 'yoh' or a 'hi', followed by their first name. Older people are too quick to regard this more informal manner of address as lacking in respect, while their younger colleagues see it as a genuine enquiry after their well-being, rather like: 'Hello, how are you doing?' If you force a younger person to use an outmoded, hierarchical, respectful form of address, this can sometimes lead to conflict.

In family circles, you would hardly expect nephews and nieces to say 'Thank you, Mr. Jones' to Uncle Frank. And yet there is still mutual respect. Youngsters regard the people in their environment as individuals, not as figureheads. And the same applies to their leaders. The fact that the boss is higher up the hierarchical ladder does not mean – in their eyes, at least – that he is worth more as a person than they are.

The Hay Group nicely articulated the challenges of leadership 2030 in their report 'Building the new leader'.

Young people have a de-fragmented approach to life. This is diametrically opposed to the fragmented attitudes of their elders. Young people are irritated by the old white-and-blue-collar mentality, which says that someone is 'better' simply because he wears a jacket and tie to work. For young people, a person's worth has nothing to do with the way he/she dresses. As an 'oldie', once you learn to understand and accept this more youthful perspective, all kinds of doors will open for you. The youngsters will be happy to have you along in team situations, will listen to what you have to say about your past experiences, and will show themselves more than willing to learn.

If the different generations learn to understand each other better and if we can all learn to accept the need for inter-cultural tolerance, the problems of our future leaders will be made that much easier. In particular, older employees who are prepared to embrace change and are willing to listen to their younger colleagues will make it easier to force the breakthrough we so badly need. But one thing is certain: if we all keep to our entrenched positions, we will not be able to move forward. Not even a centimeter.

Act VII

How do you become a good leader?

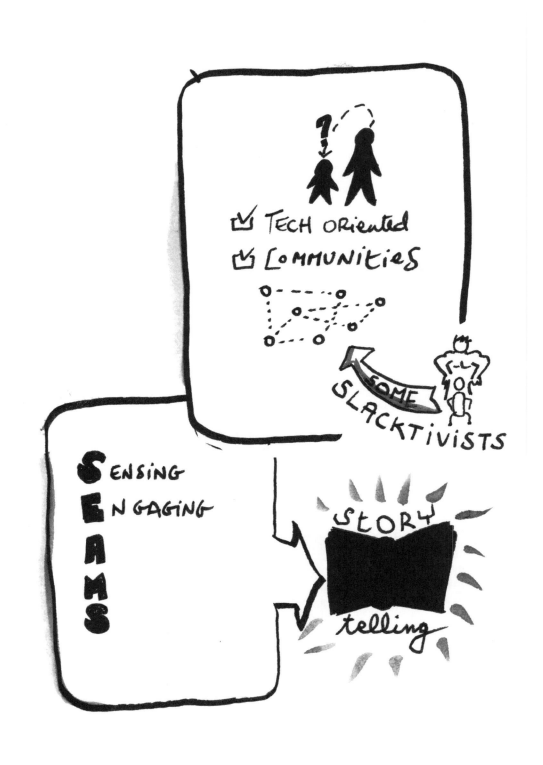

The rear-view mirror

With her book *The Top Five Regrets of the Dying: A Life Transformed by the Dearly Departing*, the Australian nurse Bronnie Ware has given us a fascinating account of her many years of experience with the sick and dying. She describes how people look back on the lives at the moment of their ultimate departure and records what they say about the things they would like to have done differently. It is a poignant story about the things that matter when the only thing you can still do is look into life's rear-view mirror. Bronnie has made her own top-5 list of regrets that people told her as they approached their end:

1. I did it (or didn't do it) my way.
2. I shouldn't have worked so hard.
3. I should have expressed my feelings more; I had an average kind of life.
4. I should have kept in contact with old friends.
5. I wish I had been happier.

No further comment is required. I would recommend that you take note of these five sentences, so that you don't need to say the same when your time comes. Make yourself a personal plan to avoid these pitfalls. And who knows? Perhaps it might also help you as a leader to realize that there are always ways of doing things differently. Or are you planning to wait until the cancer strikes or you have already had your first heart attack? Or until someone you love has already died. By then, it will be too late. If you are going to do something about the 'rat race' and 'the system', do it *now*!

Bronnie Ware worked for many years as a palliative care nurse. She registered the last words of the dying and gathered them together in 'Inspiration and Chai'. This blog became so popular that a book followed. Why not take a look at Bronnie's website. You won't regret it!

Every leader worth the name should be thinking about the really big questions in life. It is a brilliant idea (and a great experience – believe me, I know) to talk about these things in a group seminar: not just philosophizing and reflecting, but planning how you can work towards putting your thoughts into practice. And I am certain that you will reach a number of important conclusions for yourself: where am I now; where do I want to go; what do I want to do; what do I not want to do…?

The tree of life

'Change your questions, change your life.' This is the philosophy of life expounded by Marilee Adams, beautifully described in her book of the same name; a book that was given to me as a present by a close friend of mine, Dirk. Thanks buddy! On Amazon I found a copy of this book (paperback version, 2004) on sale at the ridiculous price of $ 0.68. Talk about a bargain! Less than half a euro for a book that will teach you how to ask the questions that can change your life for the better.

'Change your questions, change your life' offers advice about the best way to change a judgemental mindset into a learning mindset.

Asking the right questions is crucial. Being aware, knowing what is good in your life and who is responsible for that goodness, knowing what is wrong in your life and whose fault it is. And then drawing the right conclusions.

- *When did your life take a turn for the better?*
- *When did things turn sour?*
- *What were the causes?*

One of the exercises I like to do with leaders is called 'the cycle of life'. It is really a matter of placing all the positive and negative experiences in your life onto a timeline. Not a classic timeline, but one with offshoots, as in the following drawing:

changes of life

It is a simple exercise; you can easily do it for yourself, either for your personal life or your professional life. It gives you clear insights into the major changes that have taken place in the course of the years, allowing you to give these key events their proper place in your life story.

This is what you do:
- *Take a blank sheet of paper and draw a herring bone pattern.*
- *Write in your date of birth of the left and on the right your expected age of death (in normal circumstances: let's say 80 years).*
- *Think back through your life and note the positive experiences/events above the line; all the most crucial things that have had a beneficial impact on your personal development.*
- *Underneath the lines note the negative experiences/events in your life; the things that have had a less beneficial effect or have brought about undesired changes.*
- *Think about both sets of events; take your time; above all, write down what you feel! This will give you a visible and tangible picture of your life, with all its happiness and sadness, successes and failures, the things you wanted and the things you didn't want. Le chemin de ta vie.*

When, from the end of 2008 until well into 2009, I was given the task of helping 800 or so Belgian bankers through the troubled waters of the financial crisis, we all completed this same 'cycle of life' exercise.

If the feelings that came to the surface during the exercise were poignant, even harrowing, then the further conversations in our 121 coaching sessions were liberating for many of the participants. The words that the bankers used to describe their emotions when their banks collapsed do not lie: sadness – loss – anger – rage – betrayal – uncertainty – incomprehension – insecurity – resignation – apathetic – injustice – waiting – fear – tiredness – poor health – relief – discomfort – frustration – loss of face – confrontation – guilt – repetition – stress – disappointment… For the majority, it had a healing effect.

During these sessions, the bankers became people again. They pealed their onion, step by step, layer by layer, and rediscovered themselves. But it was a process that took some time.

One of the bankers I met during the sessions decided to change his life completely, and so he became a coach. He combined a wide experience of the world with a great deal of passion, charisma and enthusiasm. He is now a well-established and much respected figure in professional circles – and a much more contented man. Happy Alex! Love the guy!

Dirk is another one. He was once the CEO of a large international company, but was maneuvered out of his job by a rival. He took a sabbatical to find his bearings and also decided to retrain as a coach. Great, man! Today, he has returned to his first passion: music. He worked hard for two years to rediscover himself, but has finally climbed out of the hole he was in – and how! Looking in the rear-view mirror works. By bringing the negative experiences in your past life into focus, you can better learn to accept them and draw the right conclusions from them. Stopping to think about negative experiences can open the door to evolutions that can give a positive impetus to the rest of your life.

Who are you?

If you see yourself in the role of an ethical leader of the future, you must first ask yourself a number of fundamental questions. You must also take sufficient time to think carefully about your answers.

The first and most fundamental question of all is this: *Who are you?*

But be careful. An answer that describes your background, career, hobbies, family situation, etc. is not enough. Not by a long way. No, who are you really? What do you stand for? What things are important for you? What are your good and bad points?

Whether we like it or not, we all have our blind spots. It is a challenge to discover what they are and why we have them.

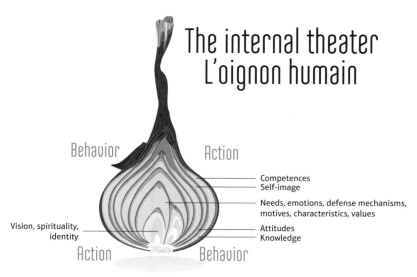

The internal theater
L'oignon humain

Behavior   Action

Competences
Self-image

Needs, emotions, defense mechanisms,
motives, characteristics, values

Vision, spirituality,
identity

Attitudes
Knowledge

Action   Behavior

You can compare a person with an onion. The outer skin is hard, difficult to penetrate. But once you start peeling off the successive layers, the onion becomes softer and softer, until you eventually reach the core in the middle. Only then can you really look at yourself openly and honestly in the mirror.

- Who are you really?
- Do you know yourself?
- Do you know what you are?
- What do you stand for?
- What is your internal theatre?
- Why do you behave the way you do?
- What are your values?
- What shaped your personality?
- Do you recognize your four different children in yourself?
- Do you know your parent types?
- Can you control them?
- Which of your childhood traumas still bother you?
- What do you think are the important things in life?
- What is your world view?
- Who are the great inspirational examples in your life?
- Heroes?
- What are the different layers of your onion?

Do you really think that none of today's modern leaders are following therapy? Or that followers are the only people who really need such therapy? Nonsense! In the United States almost everyone has their own personal 'shrink' (I exaggerate of course, but you know what I mean). It is only in Europe that we are more reluctant to talk about 'mental health'. Almost as if anyone who is following therapy of any kind must be a raving lunatic, capable of the most strange and unacceptable behavior. However, the truth is that many people visit a therapist to actually find themselves, to discover who they really are. But rather like 'outing', to say that you are visiting a psychiatrist or a psychologist is simply 'not done'. Having a personal coach, that's a different matter. It sounds chic and people accept the idea much more readily. In reality, however, it is precisely the same thing.

But be on your guard! Nowadays, almost anyone can call himself (or herself) a coach. Even though many of them have only followed a two-day course in 'therapy'! This type of coach can cause a lot of damage – and not only to your wallet. They are psychologically unskilled and often do their coachees more harm than good. This does not mean, of course, that there are no good coaches. There are. Lots of them. So make sure you find one of these. But also make sure that both you and your coach know where the boundary lies between coaching and psychoanalysis.

Why do you want to be a leader?

Answering the following questions requires a great deal of personal insight.

- *What are your motives for wanting to lead?*
- *Why do you think that you would be a good leader?*
- *What pathway do you wish to follow to achieve your leadership ambitions?*
- *Why do you think that you would be a better leader than the others?*
- *Why do you want to change things and influence people?*
- *What are your intrinsic and extrinsic motivators?*

There are whole libraries full with the books that have been written about leadership, but the essence of the matter is to be found in the internal theatre that is played out within your own self; in the different layers of your personal onion; above all in that deepest, innermost layer. The rest is just external behavior, keeping up appearances. *'The Bouquet residence, the lady of the house speaking!* There is a little bit of Hyacinth in all of us.

Manfred Kets de Vries tells the story of the changes that the leadership style of Alexander the Great underwent in the course of his life, from his early triumphs to the fall of his empire.

If you want to know if you are a born leader or can at least become one, you should read the thoughts of Manfred Kets de Vries on this subject. He has answered the questions 'What makes someone a great leader?' and 'Are you born as a leader or is it something that you can learn?'. He did this by using a fresh and innovative approach to dissect and analyze the leadership of Alexander the Great. It resulted in deep and fascinating insights about the psycho-dynamics of that particular type of leadership.

Are you happy?

During my lectures I often ask the following question.
- *'How do you feel when you get up in the morning, before you go to work?' Is it: 'Shit, another boring day at that fucking office!' Or is it 'Yes! Let's go! I'm really looking forward to seeing all my great colleagues and am really up for that meeting!'*
- *Are you happy in what you do?*

This quickly leads on to another question:
- *Do you exude warmth and happiness or do you radiate coldness and aggression?*

There is no middle way. It is one thing or the other. People either feel happy or unhappy. And if the boss is unhappy, if the boss feels frustrated, awkward or irritated, if the boss takes his negative emotions to the meeting table, then you can be sure that all this negativity will be transferred to his colleagues. Negative emotions in one person always induce negative emotions in other people. Positive feelings do exactly the opposite. As a leader, you have the power and position to influence others. But this means that you also have a responsibility to protect your people from your own ill-humor.

Here are some more questions you might like to consider.
- *What are the pitfalls you face as a leader?*
- *Is hierarchy important to you?*
- *Do you prefer to stand above people or amongst people?*

The good news is that your level of happiness is something that you can determine yourself – at least up to a point. According to Stephen Covey, the man who investigated the importance of trust in organizations, you may not always be able to control events, but you can at least control your reaction to those events. More specifically, as a person you can always choose between a positive or a negative reaction to an event. Negative reactions have a domino-effect in your environment, setting off a chain reaction of negative emotions in others. In other words, your bad mood might result in everyone around you also having a lousy day. But it doesn't have to be this way. There is always a choice between different scenarios. If someone criticizes you, you can either soak up the criticism like a sponge or you can let it run off you, like water off a duck's back. The first option leads to irritation and stress, and may disturb your working relationships. The second option means that you – and those around you – can still enjoy a carefree day.

As a leader, you also have a choice. You can try and dominate your staff with a command-and-control approach, acting like some kind of frustrated drill-sergeant. In this manner, you can certainly goad people into action – in the short term. They will do what they are supposed to do, but no more. They will follow your orders, but not ask questions – even if they are necessary. This is not a recipe for happiness in the workplace. Alternatively, you can opt to be friendly and good-humored with your people, listening to what they say and trying to imagine what they feel. You support them in their work, making things easier for them where you can. And they appreciate this. It makes them happy. And one thing is certain: happy workers are more efficient and more productive workers. Unhappy workers are often sick and are not much use when they aren't.

I regularly see work environments that would make any normal person depressed and I see others where my first reaction is: 'It looks like fun here!' And sometimes I see work environments that look like a shambles, but where the atmosphere is really great. Created by positive and inspirational leaders and resilient and enthusiastic followers.

In Great Britain I once visited a chain of food factories where the management and the staff cooperate in harmony. Where the atmosphere is calm and it is fun to work. Both sides understand each other and this has led to a strong bond of mutual respect. So you see, it is possible, even in a food factory. No strikes, no fights, no conflict models like in Belgium; just a harmonious consensus. It is great to walk through a factory like that, where everyone gives you a wave or a friendly word, and where the managers agree to stick by the rules, no matter how stringent they might be.

It was here that I once saw an ordinary worker step up to a manager and ask him to put on a beard net. The manager had simply forgot and apologized for this oversight in a normal, human manner. Everybody happy. No irate reaction from the manager along the lines of: 'Who the hell do you think you are, telling *me* what to do?'. No, nothing like that. No problem, no conflict. Just acceptance of the rules. (By the way, they also make great muffins!)

These are the type of people who wake up with a good feeling on a Monday morning. A feeling of working together at something positive and being part of a community. A community where people care for each other and take their responsibilities seriously, but without arrogance, greed or narcissistic behavior. Just ordinary human beings, acting normally.

Are you liked?

If you want to know whether you inspire happiness or misery on the work-floor, the answer to the following question will help you to find out.
Do your staff like you?

This is a question you need to ask yourself regularly. And whatever the answer, you need to investigate the reasons why.

It is also useful to ask yourself which of your staff like you, and which do not. And once again: don't forget the 'why'.
Do people want to work with you or do they have to work for you?

If they like you, this will be because your ways of working are similar. There will be a less good match with the working styles of those who dislike you.

As a leader, it is always possible to avoid irritation. How? By recognizing the work styles of different people, so that you can place their actions and reactions in a proper context, thereby avoiding emotional reactions of your own. Putting yourself in the other person's shoes in this manner is one of the key skills a leader needs to possess. You need to identify the type working relationship you are in and adjust your work style accordingly. The more aware you are of your own social work style and the better you are able to identify the work styles of others, the easier you will find it to collaborate successfully. The four-leafed clover of Robert Bolton and Dorothy Grover Bolton can also help you.

Bolton and Bolton defined four basic social work styles: the controller (dominating), the thinker (analyzing), the collaborator (facilitating) and the motivator (pushing). These four styles are further divided into two categories. The first makes a distinction between people-oriented and task-oriented. The second between dominant and compliant. The controlling style is task-oriented and dominant. The facilitating style is people-oriented and compliant. The thinker is task-oriented and compliant. And the motivator is people-oriented and dominant.

There are various tools that can help you to acquire self-insight or assist you to identify the needs of your staff. (Insights Discovery, Myers-Briggs Type Indicator, etc.). The starting point is always that organizations and people can gain in strength by recognizing and valuing their differences. These tools are based heavily on the work of the Swiss psychiatrist and psychologist Carl Gustav Jung, who believed that there are four basic types of human personality. According to Jung, everyone drifts between thought and feeling, perception and intuition. But one of these functions is always dominant and it is this function that determines a person's personality type. This is supplemented by the psyche, which can either look outwards (extrovert) or inwards (introvert).

Social media and the internet make the world transparent. Everyone is a reporter. Nothing or no one can remain hidden. This applies equally to leaders. So don't kid your people and don't kid yourself.

The question 'Why do people appreciate you?' can also be applied to organizations. In today's economy, the image and charisma of the boss (or bosses) usually determines the image and charisma of the company and/or brand. Thanks to the internet, social media and the mediatization of society every company now lives in a glass house. The new transparency of the outside world and the ease and openness with which people communicate are both features that the public now expect of companies. Companies no longer have anywhere they can hide. Moreover, young people who have grown up with social media do not understand why they should have to put this social activity to one side during working hours. For them, social media are just a normal part of life, both in and out of work. This is something that companies must learn to accept – if they don't want to lose their younger staff. Clever companies can actually exploit the trend by recruiting media-skilled youngsters, who can then strengthen the company's position in the media landscape. They know the tools, the usages and the language. They have the feeling for what is in and what is out. But the big question remains the same: are the people at the top willing to accept this and make it possible?

Are you sure you don't fancy yourself too much?

I have already mentioned it: we all have a little bit of narcissism in us. And a healthy dose can do us no harm. In fact, we need it to feel good about ourselves and good about life. It also helps us to be creative and visionary, allowing us to seize our opportunities when they come. But too much self-admiration can only cause you harm.

Do I have narcissist tendencies?

I can already see some of you raising your eyebrows. Even so, it is still useful to ask the question:

As a leader, you can carry out a simple test to find out the answer to this question. If you discover that you are the biggest narcissist since Narcissus himself, then all I can do is recommend that you seek help urgently. Your environment will certainly suffer as a result of your behavior. That might mean your family, your friends (if, as a narcissist, you actually have any), your colleagues, your team, your company, your organization, your land…

It is perhaps a good idea for leaders to read more about narcissism. Type in the word on Google and you will have a whole worldwide library at your disposal. There are even lists of narcissists that you can show to your family, friends and colleagues. Or why not make your own list of the top-5 most narcissist leaders that you have collectively experienced? Now wouldn't that be fun!

Criteria for good leadership

In my leadership workshops and coaching courses during the past 25 years I have always, always asked the following question:

• *What are the criteria for a good leader?*

The collected answers through the years have provided me with quite a long list. In fact, a list of 60 different qualities that a leader could or should possess.

These workshops were attended by managers, leaders and other responsible officers who wanted to learn more about inspirational leadership. In other words, I have been able to conduct a life-long trial in the field, involving more than 2,000 test subjects, who formulated these 67 criteria themselves.

The criteria can be divided into two groups: a group with criteria that are more or less 'rational' (management-oriented) and a group that are more or less emotional. This resulted in the following chart:

The collective criteria are a good basis for checking your own leadership skills. In which areas are you strong? In which areas do you still need to improve?

This is how we organize our sessions. Through peer coaching we give the 'leaders' an assignment that will separate the weak points from the strong, allowing us to see where they most need to focus their attention. From this personal assessment, we will pick 12 'toppers' from their list of criteria and 6 'could-do-betters'. These last six are made the subject of an action program, tackled in order of priority over a period of 12 months. The action program is supported with extra coaching sessions or peer-to-peer sessions at distance.

This can lead to self-insights. And self-insights, looking in the mirror, learning about your true self, is a precondition for any improvement. People are

LEADERSHIP RATHER EMOTIONAL

- Is forward-thinking / Has a vision of the future
- Is assertive
- Possesses emotional stability
- Sets a good example
- Openly admits mistakes
- Is not a power-seeker
- Has good self-knowledge and people-knowledge
- Shows empathy
- Has a sense of humour
- Exudes confidence

- Possesses controlled self-respect
- Guides
- Coaches
- Resolves conflicts
- Participates
- Is convincing and determined
- Shows humility
- Is enthusiastic / passionate
- Is stress-resistant
- Has a positive attitude / charisma
- Is honest

- Is intellectually and emotionally well-developed
- Is punctual
- Maintains a good life-work balance
- Offers opportunities for working
- Has good team spirit
- Defends the team
- Is a motivator / stimulator
- Delegates / gives opportunities
- Shows appreciation

LEADERSHIP RATHER RATIONAL

- Plans carefully
- Develops strategy
- Possesses organizational ability
- Is result-oriented / action-oriented
- Is an analytical thinker
- Corrects
- Controls
- Is a good time manager
- Takes calculated risks
- Thinks creatively

- Accepts responsibility
- Makes choices
- Is proactive
- Develops networks
- Works accurately
- Has discipline and self-discipline
- Is change-minded
- Communicates information
- Is open, a good listener
- Organizes / leads meetings
- Is accessible

- Makes things clear
- Gives feedback
- Has good product-knowledge
- Adopts consistent policy
- Displays adult behaviour
- Is thrifty
- Is ambitious
- Is practically-minded
- Is a problem-solver

willing to change and to modify their behavior, providing you allow them to conduct their own voyage of personal discovery, so that they can find their own solutions, rather than having solutions imposed from outside.

On the basis of such self-insight experiences, additional literature studies, chance and non-chance meetings and conversations, we have reduced the criteria for good leadership to a list of 20 competencies. We have called this definitive list the CINDEX.

WHICH META CHARACTERISTICS/COMPETENCIES 2.0 FOR THE FUTURE
CINDEX 2020

- Has a clear vision,
- Sets priorities,
- Remains focused on the solution
- Is socially competent
- Is Multi-cultural & generationally flexible
- Is a Global thinker
- Is a passionate optimist
- "MUST" → "WANT" → "MAY"

- Collaborates across boundaries
- Personal Responsibility
- Is a true team builder
- Is focused on excellence
- Is the personification of values
- Shows her/his weaknesses and is humble
- Creates an employee-centric organization

- Doesn't suck up to the higher hierarchy
- Displays no hubris or narcissistic behaviour
- Is committed and has fun
- Respects the common rules/disciplines
- Thinks equal in being different in responsability

This index can be translated easily into every working environment. The CINDEX is our guide for the building of excellence leadership in companies.

Excellence leadership is a conscious part of the architecture of human performance policy. You don't need major studies or research projects to make this come alive in your own work environment. Kouzes & Poser, at the start of their 1983 investigation into this subject, also made use of 'ordinary people' to establish the factors that were important for successful companies and superstar-leaders…

For more information about excellence leadership, please check here.

My ultimate dream is to persuade companies that instead of drawing up functional competency profiles they should rather be focusing on leadership profiles, based on competencies and indicators that would place the leader in centre stage, and not the functional managers. Companies and organizations badly need a well considered leadership architecture to increase the happiness factor of their staff, so that people will work for them not only to earn their living, but because they want to, and because it makes them feel good. This is perfectly possible. There are dozens of successful examples. It is only a question of recognizing this fact, wanting it enough, and having the courage to do something about it.

THE BIG
BAD
BOSS
ERA
IS
OVER

The world in which we live, with all it organizations, enterprises, consultative bodies, processes and structures, needs a new form of leadership, a new archetypical leader. This realization is spreading day by day. It is creating a collective awareness that can no longer be ignored or resisted.

We live in a dualist world.

At one extreme we have the representatives of the old-style leadership, rooted in the old selfish economic model of profit for profit's sake. These are the upholders of the established order, the men with 800 dollar suits and a platinum credit card. The 'big bad bosses' of the past and the exhausting micro managers of today, leading just for themselves, without the slightest thought for others and for future generations. Self-evidently, they want to perpetuate the status quo, since this has brought them position, power, riches and success.

At the other extreme we have the representatives of the new, sustainable, peer-to-peer society, which can count on ever-increasing popular support. Entrepreneurs, politicians and scientists, all of whom in their own way want to set new boundaries, are looking for solutions that well help to alleviate the major problems facing the world. They are making plans for an optimistic future, for an economy where work is fun and people stand central. These are holistic-thinking leaders, who are guided by respect, trust, generosity, balance, charisma, warmth and humility.

The old style of leadership thinking has brought our world to the situation in which it finds itself today. This is a situation that is no longer sustainable. Not for mankind and not for the world. Our wealth and prosperity have been bought at a price. It is simply not possible to extend our Western manner of production and consumption over the entire planet. In recent decades our economies have all grown. We all have 'more' than in the past and we all live longer. On the other side of the coin, we have never worked harder and there has never been so much stress and uncertainty. Likewise, the difference between the 'haves' and the 'have-nots' has never been so great. Nor has the happiness of future generations ever been in such great danger.

The earth will survive, even without mankind. Can we afford to keep on making the same mistakes? Can we afford to always be thinking about ourselves?

The new leadership is concerned for something other than itself. Instead, it is focused on the environment and on people. Modern leaders are facing the urgent challenge of turning their backs on the old style of leadership and ushering in a new era of balance. Instead of placing their emphasis on facts and figures, they must concentrate on human beings, on people rather than 'employees'. Organizations and companies need more empathy, fairness, trust, long-term thinking and inclusion.

The 64,000 dollar question is, of course, whether we can reconcile the best of the old growth model with a completely new manner of leadership thinking. A combination of the old and the new as a balanced whole. Is it really possible?

The leaders of tomorrow are currently the children of today, playing in their sandpits and romping in the park. The promotion of a new and better style of leadership must therefore start with the way we raise our young people.

In other words, if I manage to pass on the right values to my children, who in turn can pass them on to their children, then I will regard myself as a good and successful parent. When they are grown, all these children will participate in the great circus that is the world. If they then become a leader, I hope that they will live and work in accordance with the values that they have inherited, and that they will help to further implant these virtues in the collective consciousness of mankind. God knows, we need it. And as a leader you can decide for yourself. Your fate – and the fate of others – is in your own hands.

What type of leader do you want to be?
Make a choice – and choose for life!

Bruno Rouffaer embodies leadership 2020: empathy, enthusiasm, the ability to inspire others, giving the very best of oneself... He has it all.

ANNEMIE NEYTS, MINISTER OF STATE
AND MEMBER OF THE EUROPEAN PARLIAMENT

This book is a wake-up call for every leader: the world is changing and we will need to change with it, if we don't want to be left behind. He tells his story in a playful yet thought-provoking manner, but always with great love for his subject: what challenges and opportunities are facing the leaders of today?

DIRK DE CLIPPELEIR, DIRECTOR-GENERAL ANCIENNE BELGIQUE

For me, reading this book was like looking in a mirror: it allowed me to see, rediscover and realign myself. Highly recommended for leaders who are not afraid to change.

ALAIN VANDENBRANDE, CEO FACILICOM

For years I thought that leaders were born, not made — until I met Bruno!

JAN DE COCK, ARTIST

The first responsibility of a leader is to define reality. The last is to say 'thank you'.
In between the leader is a servant .

CHRISTIAN DE WILDE, CEO INNOGENETICS

Away with the traditional image of the arrogant and superior boss; the time has come for healthy leadership.

FRANK VAN MASSENHOVE,
CHAIRMAN BELGIAN FEDERAL AGENCY FOR SOCIAL SECURITY

It is no longer good enough simply to do the same things in a different way. The moment has arrived when only real change will do. And yes, you can't make an omelette without breaking eggs. But as Bruno so lucidly points out, the successful leaders of tomorrow will be those who dare to play the 'power of diversity' card. There is still hope!

SASKIA VAN-UFFELEN, CEO BULL EN CSB CONSULTING

In his book Bruno uses a shrewd evaluation of the past as the basis for meeting the challenges of the future. And that fills me with energy!

KRIS MATTHIJS, DIRECTOR-GENERAL, BELGIAN T-GROUP

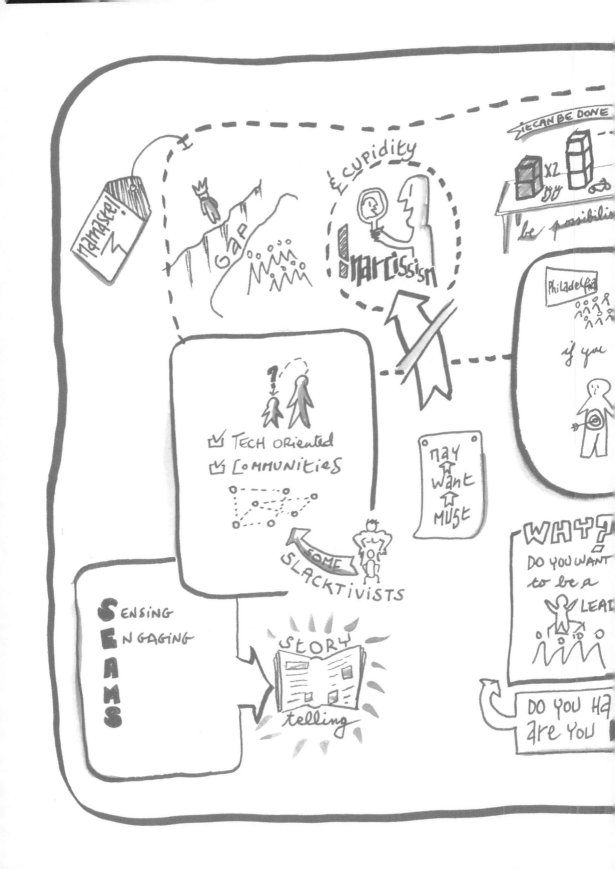